FORTY-ISH

LESSONS FOR THE AGES FROM A BABY BOOMER

Kate —
Happy Travels —
Thanks —
Joan

J o a n   P o r t e

Dedicated to stamping out the dreaded phrase:
"If I knew then what I know now!"

Forty-ish
Lessons For the Ages From a Baby Boomer

Published by Scorpio Publishing
Copyright 1996, Joan Porte

Publisher's Cataloging in Publication
(Prepared by Quality Books Inc.)

Porte, Joan.
    Fortyish: lessons for the ages from a baby
boomer / Joan Porte.

    p. cm.
    ISBN 1-888-36200-6
    LCCN: 96-92150

1. Baby boom generation - Humor   2. Aging - Humor
I. Title.

PN6231.B22P67 1996   818'.5407
                                            QBI96-666

High school picture — Lorstan Studios

Back insert picture — David Deal

Printed in the United States of America.

ACKNOWLEDGMENTS

Thanks to my parents,
John and Jean Porte,
who always seem to be there
just when I need them;
to my sister, Jean
for her patient proofreading
and encouragement
and to the little old lady
on the subway who told me
my slip was showing last night.

Contents

Introduction

"If I knew then what I know now." This is another one of those goofy sayings that every crop of newly hatched human adults vow will never slither across their lips. Unlike the eighty bazillion or so generations that have come before us, in those tender post pubescent years, we all believe that we were somehow hand picked by the gods and graced with a new chromosome that gives us unheard of genius. We know we will be able to whip through all of humanity and immediately zero in on that one perfect mate who will endow us with eternal delight; give us mornings full of chirping birds and sunshine and evenings that know nothing but mad, passionate monkey love (and who will never leave dirty clothes on the bathroom floor or order pizza with pineapple slopped on top.) At twenty, we know we can choose a career that will provide eternal, stress free mental stimulation and outrageous, teeth-numbing wealth. At twenty, we know we will never find ourselves in the position of having to do something that even slightly repulses our high and unwavering moral standards. By the wise old age of twenty, we are bottled perfection waiting to be let loose on the world.

Yeah right. Well, in fairness and allowing for the immense size of the universe, maybe all of this happens on some planet inhabited by creatures that are nothing more than giant brains running around on tiny, little, purple feet, but not on this one. Here on Earth, as twenty dissolves into life and we discover a multitude of other situations in which we can apply the word "suck", all humans eventually utter those words. And we all say them often. They become a part of our regular language along with the other epithets we swore we would never say such as, "Because I said so" and "Get over here, young lady."

The first of the many times my mouth allowed this phrase to escape, I felt a sensation similar to the one that engulfed me after a pigeon with a nasty case of vertigo slapped me behind my left ear. My skinned crawled, my teeth got wavy and my spine collapsed in on itself. How could I, a spawn of the Mamie and Ike Era, not have known it all back when I wore bandannas, strummed guitars and swayed to the beat of the protest songs? When did Father Time beat the stuffing out of me and prove I was (God forbid) just like my parents?

Let me tell you folks, that is a moment no other human being — not even the creep who makes those rolls of tape that have no beginning — should have to endure. To prevent this wretched situation from happening to yet another crop of people, I believe it is my duty to imprint on History the knowledge I now have and wished (and thought) I had then.

Oh, I can hear you. You are saying to yourself, there are History books, Philosophy Books and other erudite works all over the place, you silly woman. This knowledge is there for the asking. Oh, how wrong you are. Yes, Newton may have left us wiser about gravity, Einstein may have expanded our knowledge of time and Bugs Bunny has certainly taught us all there is to know of diplomacy and logic. But no one has gotten to the really important, life changing, esophagus blocking issues that are the key to our survival. No one before me, that is.

Whether it is revealing the secret origins of marriage, exploring the zen of cleaning, choosing a career or handling government bureaucrats, this book contains the tricks of this colossal joke called life that are best learned early. It will change the life paths of young people, improve social interaction, annihilate the generation gap and very possibly save humanity from self destruction. Or it could just result in a small, temporary dip in the sale of Maalox. Whatever.

Members of my own generation and beyond who are still struggling to come to grips with the little vagaries of existence do not despair. You will find hope here as well. It is never too late. Hey, if Scrooge can learn a few new tricks so can Baby Boomers! So "If you all know what's good for you," whatever your age — read on!

1

"Don't Brush Those Crumbs Off Your Chest"

appreciating the high art of klutzdom

~

In every century there are born a few chosen women with such charm, grace and elegance as to be the eternal source of inspiration for people who like to go around being inspired. These are women of amazing refinement who, regardless of the circumstance, are always perfectly scrubbed, pressed and shined to a "see yourself" clean.

No dirt — or other more hideous substances — dare take up residence on their shoes and sweat quakes in terror at the very thought of smudging their perfect, dewy fresh "looks like it isn't even there" makeup. These women can fly for fifteen hours on a cargo plane laden with laboring hyenas and frolic off the aircraft looking pure and perky. They can romp (they always romp) in the snow for hours and never get the tiniest hint of a runny nose. They can escape from a pit of poisonous, starving vipers after being held hostage for ten days and their stockings won't even get a little bunchy at the ankles. If they allowed themselves to ooze anything, it would be pure class.

Then there are some women who, at an elegant dinner party, lift a pinky and drip tiny specks of cream into their tea, only to realize they already ever so daintily squeezed lemon juice into the same cup and now have a wretched, curdling atrocity bubbling up before them — and everyone else — in the packed room. There are women who step out of a car at a political fund raiser, slip on the wind and somersault like an epileptic octopus in front of fifteen of the sixteen most powerful people in Congress. There are women who, just as their new boss sticks his head in her office, dump an enormous glass of sticky soda all over themselves and deep into the company computer keyboard. There are women who, at rush hour at the Port Authority Building, when dressed in a skirt and heels, deposit their last subway token, get tangled up with their luggage in a turnstile and find themselves with one leg straddled across the iron bar as seven million New Yorkers bear down on them like a pack of wild boars with an itchy rash.

In short, then there are klutzes like me.

A klutz looks with unbridled envy on any woman who does NOT run out of the house in the morning with a telltale ring of toothpaste around her lips. A klutz looks in awe at anyone who can do an aerobics tape from beginning to end without getting so foot-tied she resorts to running in place about fifteen minutes into the whole deal. A klutz can wear a brand new white suit to a two hour affair — eat and drink nothing the entire time, stand ten feet away from all forms of life — and still leave with a large obnoxious spot on her sternum. A klutz lives her entire life in mortal fear of losing her compact mirror needed to check for the crumbs, spots, stains and sundry drippings that will forever call her body home.

Let me tell you right now. If you are a klutz, medical science holds no hope for you. There are no pills, no shots, no operations that will cure you. You can even go to one of those schools that promise to make you "look like a model even if you don't want to be one." However, in a week, two at the most, you will be dribbling, spilling and falling again.

If you are a klutz, there is only one course of action. Learn to go with it. Revel in it —

breath it in! Be a klutz and be proud. Like
the great women of legend, you too have
unique gifts bestowed upon just a few of our
species. Don't do what I did and waste years
shamefully trying to become something less.
Anybody can check luggage at an airport. Only
the suitcases of a klutz will burst open on the
conveyor belt and spit up pink undies that sail
onto the shoe of the man she has been flirting
with since Cleveland. It takes no special fi-
nesse to cut up a roasting chicken. The act
becomes an art form, however, when it causes
you to call 911 paramedics AND smash your
mother's china all over the kitchen floor.

Years ago, before I appreciated the
uniqueness of klutzdom, I tried to model
myself after a woman in my office. When I
first met her she was like a beacon sent to
guide me out of my unholy mess. That she
was more than six feet tall didn't phase me
nearly as much as did her completely
unwrinkled linen suit. She had an upturned
nose, long, straight blonde hair that lay
where she commanded and she never spoke
above a whisper. When I learned that a great
grandfather had been a member of Lincoln's
cabinet and she was a graduate of Holyoke,
I knew I was in the presence of real class. I
followed her around like a puppy for weeks
hoping some of her grace would wash over
me and cleanse me of klutzdom forever.

When Ms. Class agreed to have lunch with me one day I almost fainted. I could even pick the place! (Later, I learned she was fulfilling a family duty. One of them entertained a boor once a year. It was a tradition founded in the mists of yore when the king agreed to show his appreciation to his court jesters. They adapted it over the years.) I had to think fast. Italian food was out — I could just see little spots of sauce ricocheting off her Chanel suit as I spun linguine around my fork. Ribs? Forget it. I have to be sandblasted after eating ribs. She would never be seen at Chicken Out. Finally, I suggested a little cafe around the corner that was popular with the "eat to be observed" crowd. They had salads and I knew she would never allow her stomach anything more than greenery at lunch time. It also had splatter-proof foods such as tuna fish so my clothing would be as safe as any member of my wardrobe could be.

When we entered the restaurant I felt her aura surround me. I knew that, for once, people weren't looking at me because they were taking bets on when the thread hanging from my skirt would begin to unravel. They were looking because I was with "class." Her boyfriend, Reginald the Insipid (oh forgive me, Reginald the Insipid IV), crawled into a seat next to her. This was terrific. I was going to see how a classy woman interacted with a guy too. Two lessons for the price of one and a free lunch to boot.

A burst of confidence came over me. I ordered a small salad and could hardly contain my pride when I was able to keep all of the spinach inside my mouth. That major fete was not good enough for her, however. She chortled at my choice of wine and reminded me THEY never drank domestic. (I didn't think her ancestor employed by Lincoln would have said that — in fact, I bet he snorted down a few tankards of home swill during some all night benders with Grant. Oh well, I figured classy people must evolve faster than the rest of us.) She inquired aloud where I had gotten that "lovely little ring" and commented that some people could "get away" with the color red I was wearing. My temperature was rising but I figured, no pain, no gain. Maybe you had to go through some weird kind of rite to pass into the state of classydom. If I could endure Terry Tomlinson's second grade secret rituals that made us "blood sisters until the Moon collided with Neptune," I could get through this. Besides, her butter knife hadn't fallen onto the table cloth once. I started taking mental notes on how I could someday accomplish something that wondrous.

Her attack soon turned on poor Reginald. Saturday was just around the corner and he had not yet provided her with an acceptable evening excursion. Sweat started to bead from his inordinately immense pores. He stammered as he suggested the opera, boating and the ballet. The bullets came fast and furious. "That was last weekend. Not in the mood. Dreary." The shell of his carcass sat slumped in his seat. My role model also picked contentedly on her arugula.

I tried to help the poor soul. It wasn't entirely an act of charity. I was afraid that if I didn't do something to rescue him, I would break a leg on the sweaty floor on the way out. "Hey, you know Joe and I went to the hockey game last week and then had the world's best chili dogs! I bet you haven't done something like that in a while if at all. You might want to try something different...it was really fun."

The Ice Age returnithed and hovered right over the table. "Oh, my dear, we must get you a better breed of male." There was a look of joyful pity on her face I hadn't seen since I did a half-gainer off the stage in ninth grade and landed at the feet of the class witch, Margaret Soldo. I looked at the puddle sitting next to her and wondered if she was serious. She was. Still, I watched in amazement when she consumed an entire hunk of French bread without allowing a crumb to come near her. I felt the urgent need to vacuum myself.

"But we had fun," I offered. "Isn't the point, to have fun?"

Apparently not. Then it hit me. What was the point of all of this anyway? I suddenly realized that for all my current cleanliness I was paying a dear price. My back muscles were tight and my jaw clenched, not one taste bud had the pleasure of knowing what I was slipping gingerly into my mouth. Maybe this class thing was not that great after all.

"Have you ever piled the bed high with coffee, Chinese food, the Sunday paper and then spent the whole day together in front of a fire letting things fall where they may?"

"That's absolutely disgusting!" She was so horrified she ALMOST let a wedge of cheese fall out of her hand onto the plate — almost.

"OK, and forgive me Reggie." (I really didn't have to apologize to Reginald, however. He was so melted at this point, I could barely see his pinkish eyeballs over the oil and vinegar cruet.) "What would you do if you fell down a flight of stairs, ripped your stockings and snapped both heels off your shoes right at the beginning of your first date with the most gorgeous man North of Mel Gibson?"

"I don't know. I would be mortified. I don't know if I could ever show my face again.

Anyway, how could you even fathom such a thing ever happening at any time?"

Fathom it! I've won awards for consistency in that category. Right then it struck me. This woman hadn't lived at all! If this was class I wanted nothing to do with it. Like Scarlett O'Hara, I felt like I had spent my life pursuing something I really didn't desire after all. My escape had to come soon — restriction was all around. I stood up and instinctively brushed from my blouse crumbs that always throng there after a meal.

"My God, don't touch your breasts in public!" Ms. Class was three steps over the horrified line. Touch them? The urge to sacrifice a lamb overwhelms me when I can find them! She was in the clutches of a bad case of the vapors. Other patrons were starting to look. Deciding it was better not to go on, I spun around, tripped over the chair, smashed into a post, upset the dessert tray and sailed right through the front door to freedom. Never had air smelled so sweet.

Now when I trip over a pebble, smash both knees and an ankle and decimate a brand new pair of pantyhose, I do so with pride. When I find mascara mushed on my upper eyelid, I wipe it off with a big smile on my face. The toilet paper stuck to my shoe, is a badge. A cranberry sauce stain,

13

even on a white wool dress, is a mark of excellence. (Although I understand it is now a misdemeanor in most states to sell me a garment in any color lighter than pastel rose.)

I still believe that true class does exist but it occurs once in a generation like a Mona Lisa, a Mozart sonata or a good situation-comedy on television. Others may have the technique copied but they are mocking substitutes at best. What I possess is true klutziness, which — in its purest form — is as unique and rare a gift as real class and, therefore, SHOULD be fabled in story and song.

All budding klutzes need to remove themselves from the closet, stop trying to "pass" and celebrate their innate abilities. It will be easier once they learn what I did at that luncheon — that, in addition to having talents others can only dream about, we are much higher up on the evolutionary chain then we once thought.

2

Dust Bunnies Make Good Guard Pets

the zen of cleaning

~

Hello, my name is Joan and I am a recovering addict. No longer am I ashamed to admit publicly that a harrowing dependence devoured a large portion of my life. People, I beg of you, do not do as I once did. Do not allow this monkey to hop onto your back. Don't let this habit reduce you, like it did me, to a pitiful, half human creature before hitting rock bottom. For the sake of your family, your livelihood, your sanity, I beg you, do not become hooked on — cleaning. In fact, I would recommend that no one spend more than five minutes a day tidying any part of their house. It is just that habit forming.

Oh, you may think you can go for just seven or eight minutes but it is stronger than you are. A light dusting becomes a polishing. A mere wiping of the sink develops into a bathroom expedition for spots and those dreaded mirror streaks. Life becomes an endless succession of Spring and Fall cleanings. You may see no harm in scouring the stove after waxing the kitchen floor but that is one of the key signs that you may be hooked. Trust me. I have been on that long, ugly road.

I will now share my story with you in hopes of preventing others from going down this sordid path. As with most addictions, genetics is largely to blame. My family has fought a long and mostly futile battle with what is now clinically documented as the Be Clean Just In Case Syndrome. This illness strikes many, but zeros in on the populations of most Mediterranean cultures and afflicts southern Italians with a particular horrific vengeance. It has two especially terrifying symptoms. First, there is the unwarranted fear of what people might think if they barge into your house uninvited and find it even slightly out of place. That, coupled with the anxiety over what these moochers might later say about you, is a prescription for madness. The origin of this illness is a victim of the distractions of history. It is known, however, that before departing on his trip to the end of the Earth,

Columbus made sure all of the makeshift globes in his den were in perfect order. What if a marauding band of hyperactive goats broke in and chewed up his maps? How would it have looked to have the police, the neighbors and the local goatherds search the house only to discover a messy office? Even if he did get lucky enough to find that New World, the talk of the town would surely be about that sloppy room.

You never know — Be Clean Just In Case.

This gene has grown stronger with the years and his descendants now go through even more bizarre maneuvers. My mother made us hang our wet laundry on the line with military exactitude. There would be no willy nilly mixing of socks and undies. No, no, no. We had to group socks, shirts and jammies together. What if someone decided to pop in uninvited and the house suddenly filled with noxious fumes? We couldn't have them racing into the backyard fighting for life only to stumble upon our unkempt laundry twirling on the line. It could happen! You never know — Be Clean Just In Case.

This was the same reason she made us wash the breakfast dishes before we got dressed. If someone "important" dropped by before eight o'clock, the house would have to shine brighter than Mr. Clean's earlobes. It didn't matter that anyone short of Gandhi who comes through a door unannounced at that hour should suffer decapitation with a spiraling frying pan. We had to prepare to greet Sam the oily butcher as though he were Patton popping in for a surprise inspection of the troops. You never know — Be Clean Just In Case.

To compound the problem, this was the era of the infamous "duck and cover" drills. The dazzling logic employed here was, in case a nuclear bomb large enough to make confetti out of the entire Eastern seaboard hit, we would find safety under our plywood desks. It didn't help matters that the nuns insisted we put our books neatly away as the sirens began to scream. How would it look if the surviving mutated one eyed, radiated monsters someday excavated the school house? What would they think of their ancestors if they discovered we were untidy? You never know — Be Clean Just In Case.

By the time I was on my own in college, the Be Clean Just In Case Disease was having its way with me. I couldn't leave the house in the morning without going through a spooky little ritual. This went far, far beyond checking the tub faucet for dripping and unplugging the iron. This was a psychotic quest to make sure nothing was unturned, undone, unhung-up or unclean. Dishes were scoured, the bed made, the floor polished and everything shined to a blinding, "ready for my close up Mr. De Mille" radiance. I even incorporated this protocol into my study habits. It became surprisingly easy to combine scrubbing the living floor with Geology. I found myself drawing Earth plates with globs of Murphy's Oil Soap and then mushing them together to simulate an earthquake.

It did make me a bit nervous when I caught myself spraying out economic equations with Windex. Still, I cleaned on.

My mind raced with the possibilities. What if a pipe broke and the landlord rushed in to stem the rising tide only to see a coffee cup sitting on the bed stand? What knowing looks would I get from him later as we passed in the halls? What if 12B went up in flames and the fire fighters had to bust through my wall? Surely, they would stop and look at the film growing under my dresser and you know how things like that get around.

Vacations were a nightmare. I would spend the weeks before on my hands and knees scrubbing. After all, you go away for ten days — anything can happen. My worst fear was getting stomped on by a moose in the great Northern plains. It wasn't the injury with its accompanying pain and disfigurement that I feared. That I could handle. What terrified me was the thought of having relatives come in from out of town to visit while I recuperated only to discover I had failed to disinfect that little piece of floor behind the toilet.

Once during a particularly bumpy flight I yelled out, "Oh God, I hope we don't go down. I have spots on my water glasses!" I had visions of the whole family coming back after the funeral to have that dorky little feast. Someone surely would open the cabinet and there would be my spotty glasses...my legacy from beyond the grave.

For decades the talk of the family would be, "Joan? Yeah, too bad she wound up splattered all over Tennessee. But you know she couldn't even clean a glass properly. The spots that girl left — it was a sin."

Of course, no matter how relaxing a vacation I enjoyed, it was shot the second I got home. I would open the door and find more dust breeding in the corners than Lawrence of Arabia swallowed on all of his crusades. If there was dust, there had to be dirt. What if a neighbor came by with some mail he had picked up for me? Out came the buckets and brooms. By the time I was done, I needed more time off to recuperate.

My love life suffered. Not many guys get all tingly all over when they ring the bell and find their date smelling like a cross between Pinesol and Clorox. The breaking point came when I chased a veritable Greek god out the door with a vacuum cleaner. I was not trying to get rid of him. I was just hoping to remove our footprint marks from the rug as we exited. Either he didn't buy my explanation or he knew he was treading in very dangerous waters.

That night, as I sat alone, miserably chewing a burger from the local "Yeah Right, We Use Real Meat" fast food chain, I began to think about what I had just lost — a night of dinner at La Pavilion, dancing and other forms of mutual excitement — I knew I needed help. I hit rock bottom but what could I do? There were no Cleaners Anonymous Programs available then. Psychiatrists thought I made the whole thing up as some sick cry for help and treated me for hypochondria instead. I even tried those three in the morning call in radio talk shows but the hosts, many of whom claimed to have heard it all, thought I was one of those Howard Stern crankers. I had no where to turn. I had to lick this myself.

I sat in my apartment and forced myself to watch the dust build. It was Hell. Through the shakes and sweats, through the racking twists in my stomach, I resisted every urge to clean. The clocked ticked ever so torturously. Every noise was amplified. I felt like I was in one of those 1950 Rita Hayworth

21

flicks where they tossed her alone into some hideous pit of despair. Night turned to day and day to night. I had to force myself to hang on. Every rag in the closet seemed to call out to me. The bottles of cleaning fluid looked forlorn and bewildered. Still I hung on. I even dashed from the bathroom after washing my hands to prevent the urge to wipe the sink from overwhelming me.

After an agonizing forty-eight hours, something finally triggered in my brain. The utter futility of cleaning became apparent. Dirt was always going to defeat me. No matter how far I beat it back, it would always win! Like death, taxes, cockroaches and Dick Clark, it would always be there. Besides, I had lots of friends who had newspapers on the floor occasionally and the itinerant dirty glass roaming free. That didn't make them evil. Disorganized people could be decent members of society too!

For the rest of the week I refused to wash any dishes. I rolled in the dust and dropped wet towels on the floor. I even left the house to go to work and didn't fill the dishwasher until I came home. Books I never had time to read were now available to me and I learned I preferred writing to cleaning. I preferred many activities to cleaning. Life took on a different meaning. There was a whole messy world waiting for me to cavort in!

The following Saturday, I invited the entire neighborhood over for a celebration and did nothing in advance but a minimum of straightening. It was the first time in my life I just picked up the obvious dirt before having people in my home. It was also the first time I didn't fall dead asleep in the shrimp sauce twenty minutes into the festivities. The best part was that no one cared. We all had fun. Finally, I was clean...ah, let's just say I had beaten the habit.

Today, vestiges of my illness remain. I can only bring myself to really "live" in one room. The rest of house remains absurdly organized. Organized but not sanitized. Most of the house gets dusted and vacuumed once every couple of weeks or before national holidays — whichever comes first. The kitchen and bathrooms are habitable and there are no obvious signs of vermin. I can assure you that you will get no disease upon entering my home but you may encounter a rabid dust bunny or two.

When too many people compliment me for my cleanliness I get very nervous and fear that it is coming back. Immediately, I start heaving items out of the linen closet onto the floor. If I get really spooked, I head for the kitchen where I grab a can of tomato sauce with thoughts of doing unspeakable things to the surface of the stove.

I will never know what I could have accomplished had this affliction not taken away many of my years. However, I am proud of my newly established twelve step program to combat this disease and urge anyone so afflicted to join and get help. Everyone is welcome, regardless of their ability to pay. The only requirement is that you leave your bucket and Lysol at home.

3

Answering the Unanswerable

handling stupid questions

~

There I sat, minding my own business — as much as I can anyway — having my nails manicured. This is an indulgence I allow myself for two reasons. The first is that I have never mastered the art of applying nail polish without smearing it across my palms, over my knuckles and well North of my elbows. Unless it is clear polish, I wind up looking like something Picasso's dog threw up. Second, I know I will never have the guts to do anything really up-class like get a face lift (unless someone throws a leash around me and mistakes me for his hound dog, Old Pleat) or have permanent eyebrows emblazoned on my head, so this — and getting that second shot of conditioner during a shampoo — is my big step into that magical, mysterious world of self pampering.

So there I am, enjoying a few precious moments of rich and famousness, when a guy, who works in the same building as I, pushes open the door bearing the sign that reads "Manicure Special $9." He sticks his face between mine and that of the poor woman trying to earn a hard dollar and booms out, "My God, look at you. You must be raking in the dough now. Getting a manicure? How much money ARE you pulling down?"

It didn't take me but a split second to recognize this as one of those deadly dumb questions we must all face now and then. At any given time, any semi-rational person can ask the stupidest, most godawful question ever birthed on the lips of a warm blooded beast.

Now, when you consider that many, many, oh so many human beings are fifty miles wide of grazing the "semi rational" spot on the sanity scale, you begin to realize just how many combinations of really moronic questions can come out of the blue and clobber you like cold flounder.

You have to learn how to answer these babies quickly so they don't hang out there in the time space continuum and throw off the evolutionary progress of Man. For me, sarcasm is usually the first weapon of choice. After several attempts to deflect his continuing questions about what he considered my vast personal wealth, I could see that my pal needed something a little stronger. I looked deep into the eyes of my questioner (which wasn't that hard since they were both housed on the bridge of my nose by that point), and softly and in my best Suzanne Pleshette voice said, "Ah, the travel agency doesn't bring me peanuts. It's the whore house that enables me to live this life of opulence, honey. Come on over one night, I've got a redhead who would look good on you." His eyeballs rolled from my nose and on to the floor as he beat a hasty retreat.

Stunning the little critters is also a powerful "dopey dissuader" and is especially effective against pompous jerks. One such being had trouble recognizing my complete disinterest in his every atom even after I told him I had come back from Thailand with a new strain of highly communicable superbug and couldn't be near another person for at least two years lest they run the risk of losing all gross motor skills. Finally, he could take it no longer. He had to know how I could possibly reject such a fine specimen of manhood. "So is there a Mr. Joan Porte? That's got to be it. Is that the reason you are fighting the strong desire to give into my charm?" (Desire? I was in a corner screaming, "Green eyes, green eyes! I am terrified of green eyes! Oh, what a world, what a world!")

Now, if I had lied and said yes, I would have had to listen to several more hours of blather about how I could do better than what I now had. If I said no, well God only knows what horrors I would face. It makes me shudder just to consider it. So I walked the line and hoped to shut him up for good. "Not any more." I replied reverently.

"Oh, so you drove him away too?" This was accompanied by a wink, wink, smile, smile.

"No, he's...he's...he's dead." With that, my admirer's smile and cockiness passed on as well. "It was in college...oh, it was horrible...I vowed never to be serious with another man for the rest of my life. In fact, I am considering a nunnery if I can find one cloistered enough." Suddenly, I flung my arm over my eyes in my best "Wuthering Heights" movement as though to block out what had to be dreadful memories.

"Omigod, I am so sorry. I didn't know...I never would have..." He fell over his tongue and his feet simultaneously as he beat a permanent and hasty retreat from my life path.

This is not to say that his was the stupidest comment a man has ever made about my marital status. I think the gold medal must go to Antonio. He was (to borrow weakly and shamelessly from Billy Joel) a soda delivery tycoon who regularly visited my travel agency. For weeks he tried his best lines on me such as "Ay, maybe I don't own my own business or nothin' but I'm gonna do somethin' with my life someday soon — yeah soon." (I do believe I heard Shakespeare sobbing from the great beyond at the point.) Finally, after I turned down his request to spend "Like the whole weekend in Atlantic City. Can't get no better!" he burst out in frustration. "You know, you don't wanna go out with me and you ain't married yet and you ain't no spring chicken. I think you're a dyke or somethin' like that there."

The angels themselves could not have come down from their celestial perches and handed me a more golden opportunity. "A lesbian? You think I am a lesbian? Don't you know? Oh my God, I guess you don't. You mean, you aren't gay? I mean...you really think I am a woman? Well, I was — once. I mean, wow...you don't know about the shots and the upcoming operation? I only dress like this at work.. well, I will until the surgery is complete. But it will be fun...as long as you get used to calling me John. I just wanted to wait until it can be absolutely perfect between us." I heard that it took him almost a year before he turned that old Balducci charm on another prospect.

If sarcasm and shock don't naturally leap to your lips, you can always resort to school marmishness. I once got an indignant call at two in the morning on my travel agency's all night emergency number (which rang in my house.) This should have been reserved for important matters such as being stranded in Kenya just as Michael Jackson and Macualay Culkin were landing for the month long Monkey Festival and Jamboree.

The caller woke me up demanding to know why American had canceled his red eye out of Los Angeles after it taxied out onto the runway: why I wasn't aware in advance that they planned to hatch this diabolical plan against him and only him and what was I planning on doing about this crisis! He couldn't ask the pilots, the flight attendants, the desk clerks or the darned janitor for that matter. He had to have me consult my magical crystal ball to divine these and other answers from afar.

To make matter worse, this oddball got angrier, more obnoxious and more vile when I couldn't answer his questions. I offered to book him a hotel room for the night and get him on the first flight out in the morning, but nothing would pacify him. I darned well better have a good explanation for putting him on this now canceled flight or else he would find another travel agent. Now there was a threat that just left me quaking in my jammies.

That did it. I put on my best Queen Elizabeth voice. (Which is no easy trick at that hour.) "Sir, do you realize that you are speaking to a human being? Do you realize that I have a heart and soul and feelings — that I am more than a mere dropping of protoplasm? Now wouldn't you want to reflect upon what is causing you to make these impossible demands on me and look into the possibility that there lies a larger root cause for your actions than just a missed airplane? And that threat...do you often threaten people when you must know they didn't cause your problem? Why haven't you confronted the airline? Do you fear authority figures? Do you usually go after the little guy? Have you contemplated the deeper reasons for your apparent overreaction?"

It shut him up but I did lose his business because he spent the next five years ensconced on a lotus pad in Northern Maine communing with a frog considered holy by those of his newly discovered New Age sect.

I know how hard it is for some people far kinder than I to come up with a put down or how some might worry about starting various rumors about themselves, so I will leave you with some simple sure fired ways to end stupid questions. Laugh. Don't chuckle, don't twitter...laugh — get crazy. This came to me quite by accident when I was having my one millionth battle with some mindless bureaucrat who lives only to torment his fellow human. He was all in a dither because I refused to redo some asinine piece of paper to his specifications. "You won't comply? Is that what you are saying? You refuse to do this!"

I couldn't help but imagine him on the other end of the wire as one of those cartoon characters whose faces get redder and redder and necks tighter and tinier as they get more aggravated. I mean this guy was literally spitting mad over this piece of paper. I can't imagine what he must be like when real disaster walks into his life, such as when the weather man says it is going to be eighty degrees but it only hits seventy nine and he has to cancel the picnic he has been planning for six months.

"Have you contemplated the cosmic role this paper will play in the course of human existence on the planet?" I choked out.

"Do you realize the significance of your defiance? Do you know what office you are talking to? Do you know who you are addressing?" I could take it no longer. I was swallowing my tongue at this point. I began to laugh...not chuckle, not giggle. I laughed loud and long and hysterically. I hadn't had a laughing fit that interminable and thunderous since Sister Barnabas burped right at the high point of Father Reilly's gospel on the signs of the Apocalypse some thirty years ago. In a fit of indignation, Mr. Tight Pencil slammed down the phone, never to be heard from again.

If all else fails, just stop and say nothing. I once read an article about a man who was a bane to news reporters because he simply did not answer questions he didn't like...the tape be damned. He just sat there as the reporter sweat and finally came up with another question. I am going to use that the next time I get asked how much I paid for my house or why I don't wear contact lenses.

However, the next person who asks me when I am going to settle down and get a normal life, will be subjected to the atomic bomb of dumb question deflectors. I will simply turn the tables and nail them back with an even more stupid question. My old friend, Fern, perfected this method when, at a large gathering, the local busybody asked, with mock pity in her voice, how she was able to cope so well on her small salary with those three children now that her husband ran off with a much younger woman. Without missing a beat, Fern responded, "You mean you don't know? I'm surprised since I told the whole sordid story to your husband in bed last night. Well, he said you guys never communicated anymore."

Fern started to walk away, stopped and called back in a loud voice. "And, by the way, did you know that he really hasn't been impotent these past ten years?" Ah that Fern, she always was my mentor.

4

"Did You Say Size 32 Double A, Lady?"

how not to shop

~

Depending on my mood, it is a toss up whether I would rather spend an hour at any given shopping mall or have my appendix ripped out bare-handed by an infected witch doctor three hundred miles from the most remote vestige of civilization. I lay the blame for my mall phobia squarely at the feet of my mother. (Where else?) It all started when I was sixteen and went with her to buy my first bra. YES, I said sixteen! Now, knock it off! It had gotten just too embarrassing to be the only girl in gym class (we called it gym back then) to still wear a t-shirt, so Mom and I set out to embark on one of those moments now celebrated with a fine European coffee.

If there is anything worse than shopping for your first bra, it is shopping for one when your body doesn't require it with a mother who really can't grasp the significance of such trauma. I'm not blaming her, really. She is forty years older than me — things were different in her day. At the appropriate time, you just carved out a whale bone and went on building the pyramids. Thanks to the birth of shopping malls, however, even our most personal moments are played out in a sick Romanesque arena.

As luck (or lack of it — the one thing I always had in abundance in this particular area), would have it, the sales woman had the charm and social grace of a seventy-eight year old phlegmy seaman. By her hair and makeup, not to mention her "ensemb." there was little doubt that she never travelled outside the borders of New Jersey. She would have been mowed down on sight in any other part of the world — including Buffalo. It was impressive, however, how she got her orange, polyester "flair" bell bottoms to match so perfectly with the color of her beehive. That aside, one look at her and I knew that this would be one of those days — like when I watched my Uncle Ben skin a raccoon on his back porch — that would dig a permanent imprint into my brain.

We were at the "Little Miss Training Bra Center" when Wanda Wonder Hair approached. (By the way, what the heck are we supposed to train them to do anyway — dance the Fandango? That is one lesson of life that I still haven't learned.)

"Whatch youse need today?" she articulated.

A buzz saw you moron, what do you think we need to pick up at the sundries counter today? My mother was a little more delicate in her thoughts and explained our predicament. "Youse really serious? Ah, we don't got that size here, I don't think. We don't got that size too many places...I mean like geez, who would? Maybe over here in the draw we got a few."

With the dexterity and unobtrusiveness of a one legged ostrich with a hang nail, she "flitted" across the counter to a cobwebbed covered cabinet some three hundred feet away. It wasn't supposed to happen this way. I wanted just to run in, grab a bra — or reasonable facsimile thereof — off the little tree thingie and run like mad. This had all the earmarks of the horror I suffered when my brother married. Every time my mind flashes on the memory of a little girl with large braces and larger glasses attired in a pink empire gown I can't help but retch violently for hours.

Maybe if I disappeared, Mom would forget her mission and go on to her second big task of the day; the search for the perfect birthday gift for Aunt Maria. (That was no easy feat either. What DO you get a woman whose closest and dearest companions are her bunions?) I had to escape. Even enduring Roseanna Barbera laughing hysterically at me in the locker room was better than the humiliation of the adult world. I sought sanctuary in a large hat rack I spotted in the distance...I calculated that I could easily live in that maroon feathered do-da for weeks until this all blew over.

No such luck. Wanda screamed out from somewhere in the bowels of the cabinet. "Did you really say 32 DOUBLE A, lady?" Her voice seriously threatened the glass covers on the JFK/RFK in Heaven kitchen clocks on the next wall. And as if God just had a voodoo doll with my name on it that day, Mom, bless her heart, was the only mammal West of Shanghai who didn't hear her.

"Excuse me?"

"That bra youse wanted...did you say you needed a size 32 DOUBLE A, lady?"

"Oh, yes. Joan, that's right...Joan? Where did she go? Oh, what are you doing way over there under those hats? Stop being so silly. The lady wants to know if your bra should be a double A. That's right...that's what we figured...right??? Joan!"

No hat in the world was big enough now. At that moment, I decided to join a convent, preferably one with missions in lands where the natives considered breasts wicked.

The rest of the day was a gray blur but the trauma was done. As time passed, anything with the remotest connection to a shopping mall set me off. Soon, even watching the Macy's Thanksgiving Day Parade gave me a bad case of the screaming meemies. For years, I would have to psych myself up like I was about to blast off on a seven year mission to Mars with Tiny Tim as my co-pilot to go shopping in large stores. It wasn't long before I couldn't pass through the revolving glass doors without seeing the reflection of fifteen Wandas coming at me holding out little white "trainers". Instead of drawing my attention to the latest blue light special, every loud speaker announcement seemed to be screaming out to me, "double A, double A." My mall shopping days soon were over.

The consequences were heinous. While others were reveling in weekend blow out sales in the department stores, I was blowing my budget in small boutiques. Oh, it may have looked good to the neighbors to be dressed to the nines all of the time but believe me, there is nothing chic about being able to afford only pretzels for dinner six nights a week. Even large food marts were halls of horrors and my salvation came in the form of quick shops and local merchants who had not yet joined the chain store craze. These little fortunes of fate allowed me to go wild on Sundays and add a roasted wiener to my menu. That is, if they were on special at the 7 Eleven.

Being young and strong, I could handle all of that. The real killers were holidays and special occasions. How many times can you justify giving a roll of tape from the corner drug store as a Christmas gift? I mean, you alternate, red one year, green the next but it gets real old, real fast. Of course, one year I surprised everyone with quarts of motor oil and that caused a big thrill around the Christmas tree. The gas station was giving them out with every fill up. I planned ahead and started collecting in July. Still, it takes a pretty forgiving family member to understand every lame excuse for handing them a Slurpee with a candle in it each year on their birthday.

One afternoon, I was visiting a friend who had a stock pile of these very odd looking books. Inside, were pictures of all the goodies I remember seeing back when I joined the rest of civilization in malls and so much more. There were lamps and coffee pots, dresses and jewelry, sofas and silverware all right there in my hands. When I learned that I could actually order these wonders right from the book, it was as though I had died and gone back to a life before brassieres. Giddy and overcome with the absurd belief that I would actually use it, I purchased a French, hand-cranked ice cream maker from a Williams Sonoma catalog. Soon my mail box was stuffed with outerwear, underwear and home decor catalogs.

Clothes from all over the world were at my fingertips as were flowers, cakes, video cassettes...everything, including items no store could possibly stock. Hammacher Schlemmer vowed to bring me an elephant — if I coughed up $15,000. I immediately became a catalog-holic. All I had to do was get a hot cup of tea, kick off my shoes, browse, order and fax! I knew how Robinson Crusoe must have felt when he got home and no longer had to shoot his dinner every night.

Heaven really opened when the grocery shopping service hit town. Now, I know some people have an affliction that makes them want to goose their melons and fondle their figs before eating them. Fortunately, I don't believe that particular function is necessary for a complete life. I get greater satisfaction knowing that I can fax off a shopping list at three AM and have my food waiting for its new residence when I get home from work that night.

I have even gone "on line" a few times and cybersent flowers and gifts to far away relatives. Ironically, I am not yet hooked on the Home Shopping Network but there is still hope. Perhaps, someday I will feel the need for a blinking Orca the Whale lamp — in assorted colors. For now, I take comfort in knowing it will be there when I slip into that stage of life.

Although I have recovered somewhat from my childhood trauma, I still prefer to shop in the safety and security of my living room and urge you to do the same. It saves hours and aggravation, not to mention shoes, gas and the beatings your body takes at the hands of little old ladies wielding shopping carts. The best part is they haven't yet figured out a way to stock the catalogs with pop-up Perfume Nazis.

The comfort, the time saved, the calm aside, by far the biggest benefit of catalog shopping, is being able to order something that might cause you embarrassment. I no longer have to hunt through the Pathetic Section when I need new undergarments and the salesclerk doesn't have to stifle a chuckle in front of my face. Thanks to catalogs, she can giggle herself goofy and I am none the wiser.

5

It's OK, You Don't Have to Like New Year's Eve

usher in the New Year the way you really want

~

It is no coincidence that, every year, I come down with an incapacitating illness right after Christmas. This isn't your basic case of Holiday Blues. There is no tremendous desire on my part to kick the pancreas out of every wizened, out of work jockey masquerading as "Santa's Little Helper." Nor is it an allergic reaction at having to smile every time I receive yet another chia terrarium gift pack (with the newest chia puppy included!) This is a bona fide loss of the will to live.

I'm fine during the gift purchasing phase, mostly because I do all of my shopping during one catalog-clogged night of dementia. I can get through family dinners and the inevitable fights over who has more burdens to bear in this hideous life, without seeking the companionship of sharp kitchen implements. ("Your transvestite son is living in squalor in Hell's Kitchen and your husband has a grapefruit sized tumor? Hah! I've had test after test, one more painful than the next and you think they can find the cause of this constant piercing pain in my stomach? And my daughter...well, I told her not to marry that bum, now her life is ruined and with ten children to raise.")

Even listening to twenty choruses of "Oh Little Town of Bethlehem" sung by the local children's choir can be handled without heaving myself onto one of those little pointed twinky-blinky tree stars. Yes, I can deal with the most loathsome of Christmas customs with only a minimum amount of extra strength, time released pain relievers.

Still, at precisely 11:02 AM every December 29, my nose itches, my eyes run, my fever soars and my stomach acts as though it has astrally travelled into the body of Boris Yeltsin after a borscht and vodka bender. One year I was so sick, I watched a twenty-four hour Ingmar Bergman movie marathon in the hopes that Death would get homesick and drop by.

No, the problem is not Christmas. It is that snake in the grass, hanger-on of a holiday. A holiday so insecure it stuck itself right in the Season of Good Cheer to assure we would celebrate it. It is New Year's Eve; the day we get to sit around twiddling our toes for hours, then get all dressed up in costly, uncomfortable clothing that reminds us what blubbery wildebeests we've become during the previous week. We go out, drink like people told they will be dead in seven hours, risk deadly disease by kissing every morsel of human rabble oozing up from mid-Earth, go home — with God only knows who — and throw up for hours. If you are like me and don't drink or, at best, nurse one glass of wine for six hours, you get to stand around and watch everyone else reduce themselves to subhuman form during this night of agonizing joy. Even Stalin would have had to think twice about inflicting this kind of torture on the masses. The kicker is, they package this "gaiety" into atrociously expensive, crowded, hot parties that are always sell outs. Barnum underestimated us. There is one born every thirty seconds.

Maybe I am being too harsh. I guess it is a fine day for touchy-feeling, kissy types who enjoy close contact with sweat and glitter. It's just that I develop a crawling rash if forced to kiss more than two SOBER people at any one time or be an active participant in the most serene of group activities. I was the only Girl Scout who refused to join in on "round singing." Michael never did get that boat rowed ashore when I was around.

From my earliest days, New Year's Eve caused me to incur the most hideous of bodily lacerations as I flung myself with horrifying violence over and under furniture, large dogs and the most obese of uncles to avoid that dreaded midnight kiss-apalooza. It is not stretching the truth a bit when I say I believe it will be the death of me yet.

Why do we do this to ourselves? Do we welcome Spring with this type of nonsense? No, a fuzzy, pink bunny hops around dropping eggs on the ground. For Fall we light bonfires, drink cider and watch football.

Yet we welcome the start of a new year all nauseous and headachy. No wonder our society is a delicate shell of its former self.

There is really only one way to celebrate this so called holiday. It involves the use of a king size bed, a candlelight dinner and a terrific man. Sadly, I have — of late — been missing the key ingredient to that little equation and no, there is no nationwide shortage of candles or beds. Even if I were capable of such an act, borrowing or purchasing a man for the evening would not work. For one, he has to be the real thing or the whole event becomes as gross and vapid as every other of the evening's "celebrations". Also, if you don't bid on one early enough, you will wind up with a creature less appealing than and not nearly as talented as Roger Clinton.

Last year, I finally devised a plan that would not take ten years off my already shaky life span. I refused all party invitations by telling my friends that I would be with my family. I avoided my family by switching around the lie. The plan was working when I made it to December 31 without so much as a sniffle. After unplugging the phone, I made a list of resolutions, promptly threw it out, and then made a list of the resolutions I would follow through on if I were suddenly blessed with even a teaspoon of self discipline. That task accomplished, I unplugged the clocks, killed the lights and jumped in bed with a twelve course Chinese meal, a quart of vanilla ice cream that we mysteriously crave after such a feast and a chocolate chip cheese cake. (Hey, I am making this tradition, I can pick the food.)

For eight solid hours I watched my favorite classic old movies from "Duck Soup" to "Double Indemnity." (I did have to remove "It's A Wonderful Life" from my viewing list because the VCR kept regurgitating it back to me. After fifteen playings in a two week

period, even inanimate objects have a snap-
ping point.) I went from the wonton soup to
pork fried rice to moo shu pork without missing a beat. The cheese cake was my consolation during "Casablanca." Its cardboard
plate became a weapon as I tried to snap
Ingrid Bergman back to her senses. "Can't
you see Bogie's overbite, you dumb beast?
Get off the plane. Get off the plane! War hero
or no war hero, there is no way that simp
could be good in the sack! Go for the dan-
ger!" All that beauty and not two halves of
one brain to rub together. I wonder how that
thrilling duo spent their New Year's Eves together. Now that would be a movie.

When morning came I felt invigorated
knowing that I had started a new year on
my own terms. It was also nice not having
to pump out my smoke-filled bronchial pas-
sages or wonder how all of those spangles
got onto my clothing when no one I knew
was attired in spangles. It was even better
watching the Rose Parade without wanting
to massacre the tuba players as their instru-
ments pounded in my exhausted head.

If you are on the cusp of a new year, chant
or meditate, work on your resolutions. Start
a year long game of Monopoly. Do anything
but fall into society's rituals that future generations will deem as barbaric as the ancient
Aztecs practice of tearing the beating heart

out of selected virgins. It's OK to admit you hate New Year's Eve.

Someday I hope to be able to celebrate again the way I really like. Just in case, I have a family-sized lazy Susan at the ready in my closet. This year, I am going to fill it with ten varieties of fried rice, shut my eyes and spin away. All things considered, it still beats wearing a stupid hat while a wino wielding a paper horn destroys my middle ear.

6

How To Say No, Not Maybe, Not Well Sort Of — Just No

saving time and money

~

SCENE ONE:

RING. I answer the phone only to be greeted for the fifteenth thousandth time in my life with this original phrase, "Hello, how are you today?" (ALERT: Like a buzzard marking a dead body, this phrase is a big, screaming signal that a sales person is circling on the other end of the phone just waiting to pick your bones. That is, of course, unless you live in Texas where people actually care when they ask how you are getting along.) "May I speak to the person in charge of replacing the gaskets in your copy machine?"

"No, thank you."

Pregnant pause. "Pardon me?"

"I am trying to but you are starting to make it tough."

"What do you MEAN, no?"

"Opposite of yes, stronger than perhaps and definitely on the ugly side of maybe — no, but hey — you have a nice day now."

"But I want to talk to the gasket administrator!"

"Now, now, now we have trotted down that thoroughfare already, haven't we my good man? My answer is still no. So what's your next question? Odds are you will have a better chance this time. Come on, give it a whirl! This just could be YOUR lucky day! I'm rootin' for ya."

"Uh...Oh." Click.

Now, I could have hemmed and hawed and listened to the 100 different reasons I should hear the 100 different reasons I should buy new gaskets, but I didn't want gaskets — of any kind — so why prolong the agony and waste more time?

SCENE TWO:
RING. "Hello, how are you today? (Duck and cover time!) I am calling from the Acme..."

50

"Well, now that you ask, I have this in-grown toenail that is just driving me..."

"Ah, I would like to tell you about our new investment program."

"Thank you, but I don't need any investment programs. I really need something for this toe. I do appreciate you asking. I have tried everything..."

Click.

SCENE THREE:

RING. "Hello, how are you today? (Oh Lord, help me.) Is Mr. or Mrs. Porte there?"

"No, I am sorry there is no one here by that name." That's a true statement and anyone who really knows me, knows this. My mother does not live with me and if I am a Mr. Porte then I need to talk to someone other than a widget sales person.

"Oh. I must have the wrong number."

"Yes, you must have. Thank you for calling. Goodbye."

There you have three examples of the very valuable but woefully lost art of saying no, in its various forms, and meaning it. It is one of the first words we say as babies, and we use it with wild abandon during our childhood years, yet we seem to develop an allergy to it as we age. It is amazing how many people handle this word with the same

51

trepidation with which they might face a Dr. Kevorkian two for one sale. If you want to save yourself a lot of aggravation and money, don't be afraid to use the word to your advantage. It is no sin, it will bring down upon you no evil vibration. For a happier, fuller life, get to know no.

Before you think me mean, contemplate the contributions to American productivity I made by employing this little time saver in the previous examples. I increased the Gross National Product by freeing up those solicitors to find the one person in America who really wanted to hear their spiel. I saved countless of my own hours, and opened telephone lines for other workers. Also, I was noble enough to slow the destruction of the ecosystem by lessening the amount of carbon monoxide (or whatever it is we humans spew forth as we babble) in the air.

In these cut-throat days of business downsizing and cost savings, you can use your time more wisely if you just rekindle your love affair with this charming little word. If you don't, you will find yourself inundated with "trial samples" of magazines, software, stationery, calendars, kazoos, nut crackers and other novelty knickknacks...which, if you don't return in thirty days, will cause you to remortgage your house four of five times over when the bills start rolling in.

There are many ways, other than keeping solicitors off your doorstep, that "no" will play an important part of your life. It isn't easy...some people — especially those of the sales persuasion — have developed plates of armor to protect themselves against it. Just a few weeks ago I was in the market for a new personal computer. The advertisement in the catalog for a company I shall call "Leopard" screamed out the invited words, "Free Windows 95 installed in every Toshiba notebook." Having heard that some pretty computer literate folks had jumped off large buildings to their doom while attempting to upload Mr. Gate's latest gift to mankind, I knew this was the way someone with my meager technological skills had to go. The salesman was all to eager to assure me that the computer would come with Windows 95. Fine, he had a sale.

Foolish person I. I didn't make him swear in blood to that little fact as I had seen some of Saddam Hussein's followers do on CNN just the night before. The computer arrived sans Windows 95 but with a charming consolation prize — a stupid little coupon promising to yield me an upgrade sometime before the new millennium if I mailed it back in a timely fashion.

I placed an immediate call to my pals at "Leopard". Their argument was typical if not redundant. "Wouldn't you like to keep the computer anyway? I mean, you will get Windows 95 eventually."

"Yeah, well if I keep a piece of coal I will eventually get a diamond. Right now it is six to one that I see the diamond first. No. It wasn't what was advertised."

"But Windows 95 is no good without the applications."

"And your point is? Look, give me what I asked for — a PC with Windows 95 — or give me my money back."

"Well, they aren't coming that way from the factory yet."

"Then why are you advertising it?"

"You have to talk to the people in advertising. I'll trans..."

"Oh no you don't. I have a new anti-transfer computer chip on my phone. Any person who transfers me against my will is sprayed with permanent purple die...he is a marked man for life!" (Even computer friendly type people can't keep up with the changes in our technological world so they aren't sure about this new invention and it usually stuns them into submission.) "My finger is on the button! Besides, if you are going to switch me anywhere, make it the legal department since what we have here is a nice case of false advertising. Now, give me my computer or my money."

"But wouldn't...?"

"No."

"It would help if..."

"No."

"All right, here is the return authorization number."

Problem solved...life progresses.

Let me share with you another episode in the proper care, feeding and usage of the wonderful no. I once had a lovely pair of Sophia Loren, mauve and white, prescription eyeglasses with sculpted stems. That is, until I stomped on them one morning coming out of the shower in a blind, dripping stupor and snapped one of the stems in half. I returned them to the optometrist's office and they told me they could fix my glasses with no problem. I took the salesman at his word and didn't make him come up with three definitions of "fixed" and use the word in a sentence. When I returned a few days later I discovered that my glasses now bore one gold stem with a lime green ear piece that had to have been chewed upon by a herd of teething buffalo.

"Ah, these stems don't match. What happened?"

"There will be no charge for us fixing them." The salesman took on an air like I should fall to the floor and thank him for doing this wonderful deed for free.

"No charge? This stem has been used...by what I don't know. And it's green and gold and ugly and dirty and gross. I should charge you — for the murder of my glasses."

"Oh, they don't make those frames anymore so we put on a miscellaneous stem as a courtesy."

"Who can wear glasses with mismatched stems? Don't answer that, it's the '90s. Why didn't you extend me the courtesy of calling and telling me that you couldn't find a match so we could discuss what to do?"

"Well, we aren't the ones who broke them," he huffed.

"And you aren't the ones who fixed them."

"We did this for free."

"And it looks it! Next time, call before you make these unilateral decisions."

"We can put back the old stem."

I think I was supposed to feel threatened at that point.

"Now that would have value. No, this is what you are going to do. You are going to find two stems that match and are new and you are going to put them on these glasses."

"We can't guarantee that we can do that. Don't you want to try these out?"

"No, I don't and you can give it a whirl...this is America, there just might be two matching eyeglass stems roaming around out there somewhere. You may have to punch a few numbers into the telephone but I have faith in your ability to master the technology. It is better than trying to pass off garbage. Unless, of course, you would like to appear on the six o'clock news in the 'Consumer Rip-Off' segment."

A week later I received a pair of glasses with two matching stems all thanks to my pal — no.

This ability to say no and really mean it has other applications such as at the hair salon (i.e. "I am SURE I don't want to try the purple mohawk cut, really!") and in grocery stores — should you chose to put yourself through such torture. If you hear the following words as you finally reach the head of the check out line, prepare to swing into action. "Sorry, although you have waited here through three waning moons, you will have to move to another line, I'm closing."

The correct answer to that comment is, "No, you are not — not right now. You should have told me that before you rang up the four ladies in front of me who are feeding China." Add that to a large smile as you slap down onto the counter a forty foot salmon and you have just saved yourself time and acid reflux buildup.

Beware, however, that the word no in the wrong hands is a dangerous and spooky entity. Ironically, in this age when we value etiquette as much as a buggy whip, we seem to be saying no with wild abandon to all the wrong things. You know that fine line between genius and spaciness? The same thing applies with regards to saying no in the name of sanity or profit and being a slimy rude beast. We seem to have made it an art form to put no where it really wasn't made to live.

Here's a little tip to the rotund businessman I saw at New York's Penn Station a few months ago. You know who you are. Yes, you with the chartreuse paisley tie that rests in the nether reaches of your belly. If a lost teenager should come up to you again and ask for change of a dollar to call home, the proper response is not, "Screw off, turd." Like any weapon, we must use the negative judiciously.

To prevent needless violence, I have prepared a list to compare and contrast the times when no is a valuable tool.

Good	Not Good
When a reject from the planet Neptune starts preaching and shoving literature in your hand as you desperately try to make a plane.	When a family of Amish asks you to switch seats on a train so they can quilt together.
When a politician who has done nothing but suck up to fat cat lobbyists for two years begs you to spend $50 to sit down and eat "down home" pigs ears with him.	When a neighbor is making a valiant attempt to get citizens to do ANYTHING about the pothole that just swallowed her giraffe.
When an obnoxious lout barks at you, "You don't seem to be in a hurry let me just step in here." (If you are waiting in line for more than two hours, you are allowed to accompany that "no" with a knee chop worthy of Lawrence Taylor.)	When a woman toting her quintuplets asks to use the rest room ahead of you before the children start to spontaneously combust.
When trying to talk down a "customer service" agent who can't define either word on a $1,000 bet while being spotted four words.	When a person wants to merge onto a crowded highway and the lane hasn't moved since before Loni Anderson had roots so what is the big deal?
When a mall poll taker zeros in on you when you are loaded down with Christmas gifts and starts asking you to comment on every product made in America since 1801.	When your wizened granny wants to retell, for the five billionth time, the story of how she wrested buffalo on the trails.

A few nights after the computer debacle, I accompanied my mother to bingo. (That's another tidbit you should learn with age. If throwing caution to the wind and having a night of wild abandon at the bingo hall with your octogenarian Mom is too low class for you, then you really aren't that secure as a person yet.) Across the table was a woman, born seven hours before Lincoln, who was looking for a night out with "the girls." Actually, she was quite spry and fully aware of her surroundings (a quality not present in some of my dates). She just had a little trouble with the hand to eye coordination required to track all the little numbers on her card to perfection.

She asked the creature seated next to her if she could give a hand in spotting a few numbers that she might miss. You would have thought that she had asked for one of her hairy arms. "No, I don't have time to look at your cards too. I have to take care of my own," snarled the toothless monster. She snapped her head around just in time for her eyes to pounce on the first number on the monitor located right next to the statue of the Prince of Peace.

You know, I bet that charmer bought three vacuum cleaners that afternoon just because she didn't have the guts to say no to a door to door salesman.

7

The Joy of Eccentricity

being normal isn't so terrific after all

~

Something I had always thought (and secretly hoped) was true was proven so recently. I am eccentric — odd, bizarre, peculiar, weird! I hadn't started the day looking for such a certification but it was right there in my copy of USA TODAY — a check list of fifteen characteristics that indicate massive peculiarity. If you exhibit ten or more — you are given a golden plaque in the Wacky Hall of Fame. Some guy named David Weeks actually used up ten years of his life doing a study of 1,000 goofballs and wrote a book called "Eccentrics". What that says about him may be too horrible to explore. Anyway, being a sucker for checklists (no, that is not one of the characteristics) I sat down to see just how nutty I really am.

Number fifteen was being a bad speller. Well, I am, but that isn't too bizarre...it encompasses ninety percent of Americans trained in public school since 1962 including a U.S. Vice President or two. Still, that was one in the loony column.

Next came being the eldest or only child. Nope, but even Michael Jackson doesn't fit into that category so that didn't bother me too much.

Single — was the next requirement. OK another point in my column. For once I got credit for being marriage-allergic instead of a speech!

Number twelve — possessed by a mischievous sense of humor...This was getting too easy.

Number eleven was more than a tad disturbing — not interested in the company of others. I mean I like people — sort of — well, some people. However, I was pretty sure that this would describe someone who becomes homicidal when the little caller id thing on a ringing telephone says that a windy friend lurks on the other end. It probably included someone who flips out all the lights when the door bell rings, not because she fears it might be a psycho waiting to decapitate her, but because it could be someone who wants to have dinner. Yes, and it definitely has to include someone who sits at most dinner parties waiting for the time she can go home and crawl in bed with a book and the Marx Brothers. Although I was sure it also described Jeffrey Dahmer in the developmental years, I had to be honest and give myself another check mark.

Sweat started to bead out on my brow when I moved up to number ten — unusual in living and eating habits. Maybe lots of people do laundry at three in the morning and sleep from four to eight after a nightcap of pepperoni pizza. Sure, there are whole clubs dedicated to those who eat burritos with the Letterman show on a Friday night and then write all weekend only to reacquaint themselves with the sun two hours before they get to the office the following Monday. Sure there are...Oh, what's the use? Another check in my column.

I got some breathing room with number nine, albeit small — noncompetitive; doesn't need society's reinforcement. In all honesty, I could use a ton or two of some solid reinforcement now and then but noncompetitive? I don't know. Would you call stomping around the neighborhood until eight PM threatening the dogs of old ladies in an attempt to sell the most candy bars for Girl Scouts year after year competitive? Judgement call.

Since I didn't qualify for both, I left it blank. I would wait to see if somebody else checked number nine too. If they said they were noncompetitive, I would say I was too. That made perfect sense.

Number eight — opinionated, outspoken. Check.

Number seven — intelligent. Now who wouldn't check that one? Come on, who am I — Mother Theresa?

Aware from childhood that he/she is different — reads number six. I was really starting to get into this. Maybe if they wrote a book about it, being strange wasn't all that bad. Besides, it is hard to deny when you spend twelve years in grammar and high schools that had more "cliques" than lockers and never made it into one — even as an auxiliary member — that you never fit it. When you can vividly remember the ONE time you were actually chosen to be on a jump rope team, never mind that it was in the middle of the great flu epidemic of 1965 and 60 percent of the class was out, you are amazingly aware that you don't fit it.

Number five is a gimmee for a writer — happily obsessed with a hobby. Check mark — NEXT — move on.

It looked like number four was an easy kill too — Idealistic — wants to make the world better. Card Pal (see front) anyone?

Number three — strangely curious — brought me back to third grade when, determined to find out what made those spray paint cans work, I pulled off the top and jammed a pencil into one, the contents of which were "under pressure". I had started the evening by painting Halloween pumpkins and ended up turning myself an enchanting shade of red. Of course, now my curiosity is centered on determining how many ways Demi Moore can change her face, body and hair in any given year but the basic principle is still at work.

Number two is a judgement call — creative. I mean I knew a girl in high school who carved those poems on the bathroom walls. She swore to me that was creativity in its most primitive stage. You have to admit she had quite an argument there. I mean, she rhymed her sonnets without resorting to the use of the words "Nantucket" or "bucket". However, if she could be considered creative, I can use that adjective too.

Finally, number one is — nonconforming. I never dropped out and turned on. However, judging from my married friends who spend a good portion of the day chauffeuring children to orthodontists and soccer games — I am pretty much up there with James Dean.

Well my fate is sealed...according to Mr. Weeks, I am eccentric. I wasn't nearly as upset by this revelation as I thought I would be...in fact, I was down right delighted. No one ever wrote a book entitled "Mundane People". One look at who else made the list boosted me even further...Alexander Graham Bell (who blocked the evil rays of the full Moon out of his house with heavy window blinds), Emily Dickinson (who stayed in her house dressed in white for most of her life), Benjamin Franklin (who used to take "air baths" by sitting naked in front of an open window and breathing deeply..and no, I am not going to explore all the reasons Ben would be breathing so heavily — thank you very much) and Katharine Hepburn. Katharine Hepburn! I liked this list even more.

Yes, this is great...to heck with being normal. So I was never one of Brenda Englehardt's Barbie Doll Club members in 5th grade, I am in the same league as Ben and Katharine. Besides, Brenda hasn't had any fun since the club disbanded, unless you can call stomping all of her ex-husband's golf balls into the ground one by one every Saturday morning fun.

Come to think of it, we should all work to become a little more wacky. (That is, unless it forces you to break out into six bars of "Make Your Own Special Music, Sing Your Own Special Song" at the drop of a hat.) Anybody can be normal but only a few of us can find the intrinsic beauty of sitting in front of the window, breathing heavily while wearing a white dress. That is, of course, until the full Moon comes up. Then all bets are off.

8

Happily Ever After?
Yeah Right.

why ARE you racing down that aisle?

~

Right out of college, against my better judgement and in a moment of uncharacteristic sweetness, I agreed to let an acquaintance, who for the sake of propriety I shall call Jane, share my apartment. Although our cumulative life experiences totalled the joint dissection of a karmicly challenged fetal pig in a high school Biology class, I figured what the heck. What could it hurt? I had no clue that this act of generosity would cause me to question my sanity, travel to the depths of a secret underworld and back to the dawn of time.

While I thought I was renting a room to a fairly normal school teacher, I soon learned that she was a member of a peculiar and perva-sive cult called the Testosterone-Stalkers. Sadly, this is a large group of women who although look like they lead the ordinary life doing the ordinary things, spend every spare second searching out a husband. They hold close that age old theory that without a gold band around her finger, a woman is fifteen degrees less ap-pealing than that crunchy bit of pork fried rice found under your table three weeks after your last take home Chinese blow-out.

I knew something was goofy when she would come home every night and immedi-ately transform herself from school marm to disco queen. After two or three eternities in front of the makeup mirror, she would dash out the door only to return with a speci-men that eight times out of ten, only the most generous of souls would classify as male — or even human for that matter. Among my personal favorites were the school psychologist who, with just a little more machismo, would be able to emulate his hero, Mr. Rogers; the disco bouncer who was still an Aqua Velva man and the half man-half squirrel who spent hours digging out bizarre substances from the secret pouches in his bell bottoms.

If she didn't have a weekend date by Wednesday, her eyes would frog out, her ra-dar would engage and the hunt would commence. The apartment laundry room, the pool, the bus stop, the garbage shoot; she would prowl for hours not eating or sleeping, communicating to me only with unintelligible grunts, until she had THE DATE. Sunday mornings would disappear before she finished the "Cosmo" checklist devised to see if she had any hope of roping that week's subject — no matter how dreadful — into a tuxedo and boutonniere. The evidence — not the least of which were piles of "How To Trap Him" and "Are You Appealing Enough?" articles accumulating under her bed — was mounting. No date was enjoyed for the normal pleasure one would bring, no trip to the movies was just a trip to the movies. Every encounter with a man was judged for its future payoff.

My natural curiosity and the fact that I was tired of tripping over wedding planner kits, got the best of me. I had to know why an otherwise normal woman would be so single mindedly possessed with entrapping any male of the species. I peppered her with questions daily until she finally broke and blurted out the reason behind her madness. "Well, I'm going to be able to say I married at least once. You'll probably never get to say that!" I thought for a second. She might just have me there. Then again, I would probably never say that I willingly stuck a bazooka in my right eye socket either. I never thought of either experience as a "must do".

That was it. I had to know the whole truth behind this bizarre need for attachment to someone — anyone. After hours of Gestapo-like interrogation, she finally relented. Out tumbled the story of an amazingly wide-spread, powerful cult that preys on vulnerable women who are too afraid to face life on their own terms or seek companionship for the sheer pleasure of it all. The next meeting of Jane's local chapter was scheduled for the following Monday (THE prime non-dating night) and she agreed to bring me as a guest. (She had to. I was holding hostage her latest edition of "Trap Him and Sack Him" Magazine.)

After a long ride over mostly twisting and unfamiliar roads, I found myself in a large room, lit with lavender votive candles. Covers of bridal magazines decorated the walls and white tea rose sprays soared from the corners. In the center of the room was an offering-laden altar bearing a life-size cut out of Danielle Steele.

There I found women I recognized in the outside world as lawyers, accountants, nurses and engineers. It was shocking to see people with whom I had shared business meeting rooms, seated on rented folding chairs decorated with white bows and chanting the "Ten Rules To Gaining the Golden Band."

When I could finally speak, they subjected me to some rather rigorous questioning. "Do you mean to tell us you have no desire to marry," they thundered in unison?

"Well, in my youth I could play a wicked case of 'house'. It was just that my husband was always a traveling salesman, a pilot, an astronaut — anyone who didn't come around and bother me all the time. As I grew older I realized that wasn't such a bad deal. As I grew older still I realized freedom with the occasional infusion of male was best."

An audible gasp went up. The nurse spoke. "I don't like living alone and I don't want to go back to my parent's house. What choices do I have?"

"A group house and a great dane?" I was definitely losing ground.

The computer saleswoman with long red hair and a figure I would poison my Granny's spaniel for, piped up. "I am nothing if a man isn't there always telling me how valuable, beautiful and luscious I am."

"Gosh, if I can look in the mirror and say all that to myself, it will be a cinch for you," I quipped. The stunned silence indicated that this definitely was not a good move. I had to change tactics. I moved from sarcasm to reason. "Look, what's so hot about marriage? You spend half your life trying to rope him in, the other half worried that he is screwing someone else. You. (I pointed to the engineer.) The man you are dating is sleeping with two other women and you know it. Every week you cry about it and every week you are back with him. What's the point?"

"The Holidays...he promised to go to all the parties with me. I can't be seen alone then. Besides all of my friends are really his friends."

I wasn't going to give up that easily. "And you," I said to the sales clerk. "You gave up your college dreams to become a biologist just to marry early and then he left you with a baby. Why are you still here? Haven't you learned?"

"I have to prove to everyone I can get it right the next time."

I could feel my heart racing and my pulse pounding. I grabbed one of the magazine covers off the wall, I believe it was the June issue with the headline, "Even if You've Just Gotten Your Degree, You Can Get a Man In the Same Month. It CAN Still Happen to You." "Can't you see what this cult has done to you! It has clouded your brains — taken away your free will. You Martha, you can balance billions of dollars down to half a penny. Why can't you see you don't need abuse from that alcoholic bastard? Jennie, he called you a fat pig at your grandmother's 100 birthday party — join a book club — get a hobby — lick stamps if you have too."

"A book club won't help me compete with my skinny sister, Betty."

I felt a glimmer of hope when I spotted a lobbyist who once swore to me that she was not cut out to be a mother. "You told me you never wanted children but you are now dating Jack "The Rabbit" O'Hara? He thinks ten is a nice start."

"I am sure I'll want them once I have them. He actually said he loves me. What if that never happens again?"

There were some young women sitting in the novice corner who looked barely out of high school. Maybe I would have better luck with them. "Listen to me! You are just a few years out of the clutches of braces and Clearasil. Do you have any idea what type of person you want to be? Don't you want to be free for ten years or so to go where the wind takes you before you commit to a person for a lifetime; to be with him even when his hair is growing out of all the wrong places and his teeth are as faint a memory as his functioning bladder? Once you have kids — no matter how wonderful an experience — your life is no longer your own. Think before you jump!"

They replied in unison. "We are too afraid to face life alone. We know we will never be able to do it. We have never been able to do anything right — now we will prove we have value to someone."

I practically fell to the floor as I pleaded with them to listen.

"I used to be like you. Really! I almost fell into the trap. The romanticization of marriage is everywhere. As little girls we are given Barbie dolls dressed in a $10,000 Carolina Herrera and baby dolls that walk, talk, smile but never throw up for fifteen hours straight, cut teeth or slice open their heads. But for the grace of God, it could have happened to me. They don't tell you what this can lead to. It isn't for everyone and no one should go into it for any other reason than honest love and certainly not before knowing exactly who they are first. Wait! You can still have kids at thirty or thirty-five if you really, really want them!" The faces before me grew more vapid.

"Don't you like men?" I didn't recognize the person behind this thundering sound but I could tell from the reactions of the others that she was some kind of high priestess. Besides, she was wearing a diamond tiara AND a fifteen foot veil.

"Sure I do -what does that have to do with it? It's this marriage trap — created out of fear and self loathing — that makes me itch."

I must have made her angry. Suddenly, something went very wrong — the room began to spin, women began to shriek — the lights dimmed, my head pounded and the next thing I knew, I was wondering the outskirts of town in a daze. When I finally made it back to my apartment, my possessions remained untouched but there was no sign that another person had lived there. To this day, when I run into any of the woman who were at that meeting, they stare through me.

I couldn't let it go and spent days pouring over sociological books tracing the historical origins of marriage. A few months later, I stumbled upon transcripts of a meeting of earliest Man discovered in a long forgotten cave by a crack team of MIT archaeologists. These papers reveal that marriage was the brain child of prehistoric village elders and designed as a payback to their children for those endless hours of screaming and trouble. There they sat around the cave, night after night, starring at these little creatures who somehow came into their lives in the most bizarre of manners nine months after a few wild nights spent sniffing and snorting dried dinosaur horns. Night after might, day after day these wrinkly miniatures could only scream, eat and eliminate from every conceivable orifice. As they aged, these beasts demonstrated other unsavory acts and by the time they were sixteen years old they had become totally impossible.

Distracted by the constant havoc and destruction they reined on the townspeople, the elders held an emergency meeting. Let me now share with you excerpts of the transcripts of this amazing moment in the evolution of Man.

45,000 BC
Presiding over the meeting was three time elected Mayor and Machine Boss — Og Daily. Also in attendance were his outspoken female house companion, Unga, and the village wise man, Ugg.

OG: All right folks, we called this special meeting to address the crisis of these brats who have been following us around for the past 16 years. I don't know about you but I have taken to cleaning out the T-Rex coop at night so as not to be around them and you know how gross that can be.

UNGA—Yeah big deal. It was your idea to snort those horns all those years ago. Then I was the one who blew up like a pig and had my guts turned inside out. How it happened the second time — damned if I'll ever know.

OG: Boy, you'll never get off that guilt trip will

you, woman? Now, back to the issue at hand. We gotta get these twerps out of the caves. I am starting to lose my hair over this.

UNGA: Oh yeah, so what's the excuse for your belly hanging over the top of your loin cloth? That's just too much dinosaur fat back. I tell him over and over again — it's too fatty. Does he listen? NO. If you listened to me once, just once — boom, I'd drop over dead.

OG: Look woman — ever since you blamed me for causing you to have those two brats, I have stuck around the house to help out but I am so sick of your nagging and whining...picking and complaining....

UNGA: You? You dog! I spit on your feet — pooh. I could have been something if I didn't make that one lousy mistake — one night of fun and look what has happened to me. They wanted me to be top dancer at the Sabertooth Club. All my dreams are gone 'cause of you — animal!

OG: And life with you has been a dance through a Pterodactyl festival? I never bring home enough pelts, I never catch the choice meat. The people next door added a sun deck to their cave...you're making me crazy!

UNGA: ME? What about you? Have you ever once taken me on a trip? Have you ever once acknowledged how clean I keep the cave? No, every night same old thing — a snort, a scratch and it's off to the poker games with the boys.

UGG: That's IT!

UNGA and OG: What's it?

UGG: That's how we get them back. We force one male child and one female child to live together under one roof for the rest of their lives.

UNGA: We don't hate them that much.

OG: Diabolical.

UGG: No, listen, this will be great. What a vision I'm having. We unite them in a big ceremony — make them feel real important for one day so they look forward to it and then — before they sober up from the Pansadorous juice — they are trapped in a life time of guilt, anger and unrealized dreams. Bingo! Bingo? Hey, that gives me another idea! I'll deal with that later.

OG: Yeah, I like it — snappy.

UGG: Remember, we have to get them young and convince them this is the only way to live life. The sooner they do this, the sooner they will be out of our hair.

OG: How about this? We tell them if they don't do this and have more little creepies like themselves quickly they will be outcasts and never be loved.

UGG: Good, good nice touch — guilt and pressure — always a winning duo. Remember we gotta talk this thing up good.

OG: Yeah, what if they don't buy this?

UGG: Boy, you never had an imagination. Listen to me. You've got pressure — guilt on your side.

OG: And I should know about guilt.

UNGA: (expletive deleted).

UGG: We know how insecure they are — work with it. OK, now what you need on top of that is to make it trendy. It's got to be a big, big, day — the women wear dresses made out of Brontosaurus leather.

UNGA: Expensive.

UGG: Precisely...we use Rantus flowers that have to be stolen from that evil tribe over the ravine. Then...oh wait this is going to be brilliant...then everybody has to give expensive gifts....

OG: So they feel obligated not to give them back no matter how big a mistake they are making. We brainwash the monsters into it! Ugg, my man, no wonder you are the wise one. I think you may have started something here.

And so he did.

Happily, a number of women have escaped the cult and underwent deprogramming. After years of travelling, living on their own, learning what type of person they wanted to be and really getting to know who they could and could NOT live with, many married and remain pleased with their decisions to this day.

Jane, like most of the remaining devotees, is divorced, supports two kids, travels only once a year to fight with her mother and spends most of her free time trying to get child support payments. All is not lost, however. She got her big wish. At least she can tell everyone she married at least once.

9

Give Me a Book, Mr. Bubble and a Water Pistol

real fun on a Saturday night

~

Quick! Call three married (or deeply committed for a long period of time to a significant soul mate though they have yet to formalize the relationship in the conventional manner) friends! Oh, wait! In order for this to work it has to be a Saturday night...so, if it is any other day, just take copious notes and refer to them in a few days. If you call a married friend on a Saturday night and you don't get an answer one of the following has happened: A) one set of in-laws has escaped from the padded home and was last spotted heading for their house, B) the nerdy kid down the street accidentally detonated a nuclear bomb, or C) locusts have invaded their home. Or it could be that they are out celebrating a really special occasion — like an anniversary or that they have finally learned to sleep together without endangering one another's vital organs during the night.

Single people, on the other hand, are NEVER home on a Saturday. A whole weird ritual has arisen around the planning of, exaggerating and bragging about the big "Saturday Night Event." Saturday night on the town is a symbol of the freedom and excitement only hip, unattached, unchilded, happenin' singles can enjoy and most of them play it to the hilt. Pass any water cooler surrounded by three or more single people on a Wednesday and you they will impress you with stories of the excitement that will rain down on their heads that weekend.

"I'm going to the U2 concert in Paris and then skydiving over Monte Carlo at dawn."

"I'll be at the Bolshoi Ballet."

"Another Saturday — another Broadway opening with Liza."

Dinner, dancing, galas, reveling — whatever; it seems that every single person craves partying on Saturday night!

Everyone but me. I was born without the gene that finds Saturday night out on the wild town that big a thrill. Still, I spent the goodly part of the Saturdays of my twenties and some of my thirties, I am ashamed to say — dashing off into that fun, fun world of good times, were I would have to show what passes for my perky side (and there IS nothing more enjoyable to me than perk) to a horde of closely packed people I wanted to be with about as much as I wanted to entertain the drunken crew of a Turkish fishing trawler.

I can think of lots more fun things to do in this world than lose a pound of flesh off my shins on a crowded dance floor; ruin expensive outfits with drinks tippled upon me by slobbering drunks or getting squished to death in loud, crowded, hot, smelly concerts. Still it was Saturday night and I had to live up to the reckless single and free image. If you are single and don't go out on Saturday, society marks you as a bore, anti-social, perverse, asexual or worse; perhaps even a "quiet loner".

It doesn't matter if you have a date or just huddle with a few of the "girls", you just have to get out of that house on Saturday. If you lose a lip in a crowded revolving door at another smoky concert arena, that is the price to pay for enjoying the true swinging single Saturday night.

Oddly enough, as my friends started to marry off I learned something completely shocking. I was not the only one who hated Saturday Night Madness. More and more as

I called my married pals to find out what was on tap for the weekend, I heard, "Thank God, I am out of that circuit. Better you than me! Good luck; I get to stay put now." Almost everyone I called gave me this same mixture of relief and pity. Most startling was the revelation from my friend, Christa who was always coming up with the most goofy weekend festivities for us to explore. Her best was when we crashed the Texas State Society's Armadillo Night bash at the Kennedy Center to search for senile oil barons. (This was before Anna Nicole Smith cornered that market.)

"Wait a minute! You didn't like going out all those years — even to Pee Wee Herman night at Tramps?"

"Ugh, especially that one."

"But you placed second in the look-a-like contest...and you would have won if you used more pancake like I told you. I did that because I thought you liked it!"

"Oh get real...The best part of getting married is not having to do that anymore. Get yourself a husband...then you can stay home and relax."

I was stunned. Married people don't have to go out every Saturday night. Married people can say out loud to the whole world that they don't like to go out on Saturday night. Married people are free to do whatever they want on a Saturday night. Oh, yeah, there is a trip to Taco Gaso once in a while...a night out at range practice with the his and her guns that they ironically give one anther each Christmas, yes...but once you get married you get to stay in the home you work hard for, comfortable in your jeans all weekend almost every weekend! Forget having kids and building a life together...I am convinced many people get married just to have a little peace on Saturday night!

They even developed a cutesy name for this married bliss...get this..."cocooning". Right, if you are single and stay at home you are a dork. If you are married, you are a cuddly cocooner. I'm surprised a whole new anti defamation league hasn't spring up around this blatant form of discrimination.

All the time I had wasted...all the money shot on disco clothes I didn't really want and now couldn't even pawn off on the local homeless shelters! (They may be destitute but they do have some discrimination.) If few people really like doing all of this, why were we all willing lambs to the slaughter? Is it because single people feel inferior to the coupled and have to show them they can have "fun" deprived of those shackled to children and hearth? Is it because single people are younger and have to prove they have the energy to flap around like that silly Energizer bunny on speed? What did it matter now? Like Marley's Ghost, I could not make up for lost time but only wander the Earth trying to prevent others from falling into a similar fate.

First, I had to wean myself from this foolishness — forget that I ever allowed myself to be a sheep to sordid customs. I went cold turkey and canceled all Saturday appointments into the next millennium. That wasn't too difficult since many of my fellow revelers were now respectable married folk tucked safely into their homes, ah "cocoons." It was then that I learned the real meaning of freedom and weekend relaxation.

Still, the transition was not all that easy. For the first two Saturdays at home, I dared not turn on the lights for fear it would get around that I was home during prime partying hours. That ended when the flashlight batteries failed as I was sneaking under the hallway window on my way to the kitchen and I splattered myself down the stairs. It was weeks before I stopped flinging myself under a bed when the door bell rang, however, — too terrified that the Jehovah's Witnesses on the other side would post notices in my office building that I was indeed in my jammies at eight o'clock giving myself the Cindy Crawford "Beauty Even For the Moleless" facial treatment.

Even now, I sometimes have nightmares of choking to death on a chicken bone or something similarly Liz Taylorish and as they are carting my cold, blue body out of the house, the paramedics all whisper, "Too bad she didn't go out — it just defies the laws of nature for a single person to be home on a Saturday night."

Still the payoffs are great. When you break the chains of conformity you can do a lot on a Saturday night in a big city. You can watch movies in your own home and in a comfortable chair, not one of those Louis XIV torture seats in the theaters, with gum-smacking teenyboppers on your shoulder and God knows what sticking to the soles of your shoes. You can call restaurant services to bring a first class meal to your door and eat a four course French dinner on your living room floor in your flannel jammies. If you feel really wicked, you can mix a little French, a little Chinese, a little Italian. If you have a good enough delivery service you can have a cornucopia of indigestion laid before you.

You can soak for hours in the tub — catch up on books that are turning to dust in your library and howl at reruns of the "Love Boat". Thanks to modern technology — you can "surf the net" and try to figure out which of your fellow "netters" are geeks and which are pretending to be dweeby just to start a fight. If you really want to go for broke you can dig through everything you have saved since high school (which, if you are like me, can fill Tutankhamen's tomb) and try to figure out just why you had to save that carnation from someone named Franco. In short, you can enjoy the world of mystery and fun that is your home and still catch a few rounds of "Celebrity Wheel of Fortune."

For the most part, I am comfortable with my decision. After a few weeks of quiet Saturday bliss, I began to think about just what we accomplished during those nights on the town. Most of the men we met were certainly not worth putting on an old pair of saddle shoes for, no less a brand new dress. Who meets significant others in a bar anyway? For that matter, who meets anyone we want to around in the light of day at a bar? No one I knew — we were just fooling ourselves if we were thinking that Mr. Right was going to Hustle over to us under that big reflecting ball on the dance floor!

My dry cleaning bills went down, my Visa bills bottomed out and it is always a plus when you wake up on Sunday and your mouth doesn't bear a distinct resemblance in texture and odor to a Venice canal in August. I am so proud that I have taken this huge step towards discovering the simple joys of Saturday night. Now if I can just get rid of the old lady wig and granny dress still tucked up in the closet by the front door to be used in case a married friend comes over to check on me, I would know I was completely cured.

10

Friends Don't Let Friends Drive Yellow Cadillacs

test your friends before they test your sanity

Some kids forge deep lasting friendships from the time they are in their cribs. One of my sisters still exchanges Christmas cards with her first finger paint partner in nursery school. My mother joined a group of women called the Starlight Girls when she was nineteen years old. At the risk of losing my place on the Christmas gift list, I hesitate to say how long the club has been kicking, but as my father so delicately puts it, they were "Girls" when the Hudson River was a dew drop. Let us just say that Franklin Roosevelt was still finding out where his undies drawer was at the White House when they had their first meeting.

Then there are people who think they have a friend, only to discover that she was the only person in the town Scout troop who didn't get a post card when "the pal" went on vacation. There are people who accidentally discover that her "best friend" has quite the lucrative little business going selling tickets to her parents' pool when she isn't looking. There are people who think they have friends who vow they will vote for her for class secretary and then she winds up with one vote — her own. (Got your hankies out yet?)

Despite these childhood traumas, it took a hunt for my first new car to really teach me just how important it is to screen and type people before clutching them to the big bosom of friendship. (So stone me, I am a slow learner.) It was dusk and the lighting was a bit skewed. The car of my dreams was before me, perfect in all of those very important and highly technical automotive categories — it was small enough, cute enough, had AC and was cheap enough. There was one small problem. The color looked a little, well a bit on the metallic side. All right, the car looked like it was the love child of R2D2 and a neon sign marking a Broadway cathouse.

It was the last one on the lot and I really liked the way I looked behind the wheel. "It's not really metallic looking, it's just the lights," my friend said with the MOST encouraging smile. "Look at the cute pocket for your junk right on the door. Oh, and it has a holder for both large and small drinks!"

That was another big mechanical plus I had overlooked. "Yeah but it is so shiny! I don't want to look like I just fell off a meteor coming from Venus or something."

"Let's take it for another ride...You will fall in love. I guarantee." Well, we did and I almost gave in but it still looked odd to me. Despite her encouragement to buy immediately, I decided that I would make my final decision by the truth of the next morning's light.

When morning came and we drove back in her father's '76 Buick, I was relieved to see that my "pal" was right after all...the car was not a hideous metallic but a beautiful sedate sapphire. "Oh, gee I really thought it was going to be gross looking," my friend sighed sorrowfully.

"You what? What was all the talk about 'take it for a ride, you will love it. It's not all that metallic?'"

She shifted in her Birkenstocks..."You seemed to like it so I figured...Well, I'll never get to buy a new car for years so how would I know?" There it was — my best bud had devised a rather devious plot — if I was going to get a new car before her, I would at least look like a moron tooling down the street in it.

I immediately drove home in my non-shiny new car — alone — sat down and created a test that will prevent my fellow Man from going through this type of pain. (That's just the kind of kid I am.) Life doesn't need any more complications for Heaven's sake. We break out in a sweat before getting into bed with someone as our imaginations run wild thinking of all the mutants our partners may have bedded over the past ten years. We worry that our jobs may disappear because some fat corporate suits want to merge in the only way they are still capable. We live in fear that one day some loud geek will thrust a television camera in our face and demand to know why we didn't know the man next door was gathering shrunken heads in his cookie jar. The last thing we need to worry about is who is our real friend. This little test will help you tag, mark and track the genuine thing.

Joan's True Friend Test

1. You are all prepared for the first and only trip down the Yangtze River for Westerners for which your friend had to cancel plans to attend her rich, heir-less Aunt Zelda's 125th birthday party and you came down with a

flu and fever of 106 and ruin everything. Does your friend:

A) shove your head under the tow during one of your many trips to the porcelain god,

B) sneak out of the waiting room when you are at the doctor's office (in your coat, no less) never to be seen again,

C) unpack all the suitcases and whip up a pot or two of chicken soup that she serves with a flask or two of Wild Turkey?

2. You model a dress you bought for a hot date that you think gives you a body that would make Jaimie Lee Curtis cringe in jealousy but really makes you resemble "Liz Taylor the Warner years." Your friend:

A) gushes over what a "knock out" you will be in the dress,

B) mumbles "That's a humdinger of a dress" and races out to guzzle Diet Coke,

C) pulls out the sales slip, throws a large coat over you and drags you back to the store.

3. You are dating a guy who you know was divorced once. Your pal knows that once was not enough for this Henry VIIIth wanna-be and that he is really down two wives and currently sharing his out of state home with another long time love. She:

A) lets the little tidbit slip at lunch attended by four other women just as you are in the act of swallowing a sharp edged raw carrot,

B) says nothing and watches you break off piece after piece of your heart and hand it to the baboon,

C) sits you down alone and says, "You may hate me but..."

4. You mention in passing that you would rather eat moldy rutabagas on seven grain, four rock bread every day for the rest of your life than help chaperon your sister's kid's sixth birthday party but you really have no choice. Your pal:

A) cuts you off before the words "seventeen six year olds" finish escaping from your mouth with the announcement that she just joined the Shakers and you know how they are about children,

B) laughs and lectures you about being a "push over",

C) without you even asking, shows up at the party in a clown suit bearing balloons, favors and those wonderful noise makers that bring parents to the brink of suicide.

5. As is your style, you fall down a flight of wooden stairs two days before Christmas and open a charming new crevice in your crania. While you are trying not to act like a sniveling idiot, the blood is seeping through the bandage and splat-

tering the floor. You aren't hemorrhaging or anything that dramatic but there is just a little too much blood to make you feel real secure. Still you don't want to go to the hospital on a weekend night during the holiday season to sit for six hours between a wino and a party reveler who came up with one too many things to do with a plastic Rudolph nose.

You just want to hear a friendly voice and get a few first aid tips. The only friend you can reach lives twenty miles away and is busy dealing with the visions of sugar plums racing through her two little children's heads. She:

A) screams "I'm scrubbing down the chimney right now for Santa, call me later,"

B) says "Gee, hope you don't mess up the new hardwood floor,"

C) says "I'll be there in a second just keep the pressure on the cut" and you have to convince her you just wanted to talk until you got things under control.

6. You married a sniveling nerd who does everything he can, including visiting his mother, to stay as far away from you as possible after you have had emergency surgery because he "doesn't like hospitals". Does your friend:

A) regale you for hours about the horrors of the Y chromosome until you deliberately cause an air bubble to form in your intravenous lines,

B) regale you for hours with "you think your husband is an ass" stories,

C) stays at your bedside for hours after work and at lunchtime listening to you and doing anything possible to make you feel better?

7. You decide to take the plunge into matrimony but have a terrible fear of exchanging vows while people stare at you with silly grins on their faces and visions of hot dog wieners in their heads. You opt for a small ceremony, with family and another friend as your maid of honor. Your friend:

A) tells every mortal with ears what a hateful ingrate you are,

B) never misses an opportunity to remind you how nice it would have been to be at your wedding, if you had found the human decency to invite her,

C) gives you a silver tray engraved with your initials.

8. Every Christmas and birthday your friend:

A) buys you gifts that would be wonderful if you were into Portuguese ballet, Dadaism or the Time/Life series of great porcupine paintings in American Art – things she couldn't live without,

B) lists all the things she would have gotten if you would take to getting her bigger gifts or if her job were better or if she didn't have

to buy so many gifts for her stupid family
or....

C) Senses the one gift you really, really want
every time.

The more "C's" you give your friends the
more you should hang onto that person and
start to work on the method to clone them.
If you have a high "B" scorer...well, you've
got to ask yourself if friendship is worth the
pounding headaches you are sure to get after a few hours in her company. But hey, everything has a price...if you are a brave soul
and need friends around to make you happy,
you might want to go for it.

If you have to score someone with more
than two "A's" and you still want to be in the
same hemisphere as that person, get your self
to analysis quickly or, better yet, start rooting
for the Jets. Make your life of pain and suffering complete.

11

Crank Up the Peggy Lee — Making Your Own Musical Trend

sing your own special song even if it is "Bali Ha'i"

~

Who is Was and why was he ever not a Was? And if he was a Not Was when did that happen — and why did he transform from Was to Not Was? How does someone be both a Was and a Not Was at the same time?

As more confusion over the subtleties of modern music engulfed me, it confirmed something I had feared — I am always fifteen steps out of beat musically with my generation. How many other kids listened to Broadway show tunes while Jim Morrison and the Doors were exposing the '60s generation to the musical joys of death? There I was at the bus stop in my orange miniskirt, maroon body suit and white glossy boots grooving to the theme to "Brigadoon". Quite a sight.

The only musical bond I had with the rest of my generation were the Beatles. Still, I never could get all worked up over that rumor about Paul being dead. So the walrus was smiling on the album cover? Maybe he had a wild time in the watering hole the night before. Besides, I always thought Paul was pretty wimpy even before he and those dynamos, Wings, asked the riveting musical question, "How can I tell you about my loved one?" (Note to Paul: the question should be why are you telling me, big guy? Why?) John's chipped tooth was more mesmerizing than Paul's peach fuzz beard any day.

After Yoko did a number on the Fab 4, I "passed" by buying some Stones records, and I can never thank the Animals enough for "House of the Rising Sun". That song still causes me to drive around the block a few extra times when it comes on as I am pulling into my driveway. (And like all good songs, it ALWAYS comes on at the end of my trip. Stuck in a traffic jam, you get fifteen straight hours of Blind Melon in concert with Toad the Wet Sprocket...pull into the parking lot and on comes Sinatra. You figure it out.)

R.E.M. is a dream state, The Red Hot Chili Peppers are what I eat in Santa Fe and heavy metal is something they used to make in Pittsburgh. I try — really — it's just that I don't get it. When I wore out my 45 of "Satisfaction", I spent an entire afternoon learning how to say "Ina Godda Davida" so I could say at all the parties..."I sat through 'Ina Godda Davida' twice!" Still, I lived in fear of the conversation turning seriously musical. Once when asked what I thought of the universality of pain encompassed by the underlying cry against sexual dissatisfaction in "Stairway to Heaven", my mind went so blank I faked choking a pretzel. Life of a musical nerd was Hell.

Slowly, I realized that others had a worse musical affliction than that which had me in its steely grip. It started with the "Bubble Gum Music" craze. People really liked jiving with "Bubble Gum Music" and admitted it in public? "Oh sugar — two, three, four — ah, honey, honey — two, three, four — you are my candy girl.") Candy girl — now there is something I have always aspired to be. "I just can't believe the loveliness of loving you." I can't believe someone had the guts to write that down or show it around when they got over the munchies.

Speaking of drug induced glazes, is there some magic power in Billy Ray Cyrus' ponytail that make people want to line up and jerk around like gastrologicly impaired donkeys while he moans about his heart? If you have a pain, take a pill but don't inflict more torture on the defenseless masses by moaning about it over and over again in public.

Then there was our beloved leader, President Jimmy Carter who had the Captain and Tennille, those musical legends, entertain a foreign dignitary in the White House with a stirring rendition of "Muskrat Love". If they could get away with that without facing exile in Siberia for life, I could belt them out with Ethel Merman. I slowly began to donate all of my socially acceptable albums to the Home for the Musically Insecure.

The day I finally completely stepped out of the musical closet was at my twentieth high school reunion when the entire room was up promenading to the fifteenth rendition of "YMCA", looking like antique Mouseketeers searching the skies for their much needed lithium. Questions started to race through my mind. What had we learned in all of those years in school together? What had we become as a people? Would our lives ever have real meaning? Would Tom Daley's shirt buttons come flying across the room the next time he stretched up his arms during the "M" portion of "YMCA"? At that precise moment it hit me (an idea, not a button.) I had to share the benefits of marching to my own musical drummer with my classmates and the generations to come.

I immediately organized a "bring your own music" party and urged everyone to bring nothing except their favorite CD's and albums no matter how socially incorrect. At first, we faced the same sounds that made me cringe years ago. I knew that I had to force a moment of truth. In a most dramatic fashion I snapped off the CD player that was blaring the latest gift from the world of heavy metal, stood on the sofa and bellowed, "Fellow classmates. We have suffered together through Mr. Frank's sex education classes and most of us — other than Bennie who was last seen selling flowers in the Village — survived. Now we must overcome another fate of youth — musical tyranny. You don't really want to 'Get down and boogie oogie oogie' into old age do you?" I was getting their attention but a few were still monkeying in the corner to imaginary muzak.

"You don't have to pretend you think Michael Bolton is actually sexy." Rosemary Malone relaxed and smiled. "And for God's sake you can stop pretending you understand Dylan!" That even stopped the monkeys but only momentarily. "Now go home...go home and bring forth your truly favorite records. It is time to take off the wrappers and gain acceptance in the clutches of your pals."

Many stood stunned and then looked at one another in knowing fear and anticipation — I knew that I was not the only one who had a musical secret. To help make it easy for them, I immediately racked up my "Hello Dolly — Original Broadway Cast" album. "You are not alone my dear friends...now disburse and bring to light the music you really enjoy, even if it is Andrew Lloyd Webber."

That did it! Like the Israelites fleeing Egypt, my pals ran from the room with the yoke of years of fear lifting from their shoulders. Shortly, more than half returned dusting off albums and tapes cloaked in brown bags and unmarked envelopes. The one moment that caused all of us to weep with joy was when Mark — the Dude — Berchanko opened his tattooed hand and handed me an old 45 of "Bali Ha'i". Later he confessed that the entire "South Pacific" score made him "all goosey and tingly-like, you know?" It was a wonderfully liberating evening that ended with a group sing of "My Way".

If gripped by the inclination to go against the musical grain — don't wait twenty years to seek soul mates. They are out there — just have the courage to make your own musical trend even it you must "climb every mountain and forge every stream" to do it.

Of course, shortly after I freed myself from musical servitude, Natalie Cole made a fortune singing the classics with her father (thanks to modern technology). The success of the record proves two things to me. One, there are lots of other people who secretly listen to good music and Natalie was smart enough to take a risk that they would come out of the closet. Oh yeah, and, she owes me a fortune in royalties since I really started the trend.

12

Beyond The Fun Steps
To Having Children

think before you procreate

~

"I'm going to kill you. Stop doing that you little bastard. You are such little bastards. I am going to kill all of you. Worthless — all of you. Look what you are doing?" That was the "entertainment" provided me free of charge courtesy of a woman seated a few tables away at the "Gag and Fly" coffee house as I sat out yet another thrilling fog delay at Dallas Fort Worth Airport. She wasn't talking to a gang of orange haired, green toothed punk rockers. She was addressing her three children, the oldest of whom was barely more than seven. Their sins were giggling and making goofing faces at each other and doing those other nutty, little things kids (and some drunken politicians) just have to do to kill boring hours.

Ten years ago I would have taken a mighty superior attitude — after all, this woman obviously was the lowest form of oceanic debris. I know I would have sniffed at her — I always sniffed at people SO far beneath me back then — and gone on my way, happy that I was not so low and depraved.

Don't get me wrong, it still took my every membrane to refrain from smothering her chicken face in the bowl of artificial sweetener (and it was a generic brand too). With age, however, comes that sick little feeling in my gut that this could have, might have, very well may have been me if circumstances were different. That's what old age does you to — gives you perspective with those crow's feet. That is Nature's way of making up for the effects on the body of gravitational pull.

Who knows her history? Maybe she makes $2 an hour sorting buttons in a sweat shop. Maybe her husband ran out as she was giving birth to the third child on the kitchen floor. Maybe she was running from a savage who beats her. Maybe she had parents who treated her in the same fine fashion and found herself trapped in some kind of weird spin cycle of unawareness. Maybe she just had kids because someone told her it was all the rage and she didn't have a clue what it entailed.

Please don't get me wrong, here. The touchy feeling — I am a poor victim so do pardon me while I drain the blood from every person on my block — drivel gives me the shakes. That is another absurd '80s invention that ranks right up there with designer sneakers. There is never any good excuse for verbally (or otherwise) abusing kids. It was just that I couldn't help thinking about what horrible turn in the road brought her to hate herself and everyone she touched — especially those she conceived. It also saddened me think how her life (and the lives of those poor kids) could have been different had she known about the soon to be patented Porte Think Before You Procreate System.

Much like marriage, society gets all goofy over procreation. Not that reproducing is necessarily a bad thing mind you, just ask the Shakers. It's just that it isn't a job for everyone. Allow me to elaborate. I have tonsils, lungs and a tongue and so does Whitney Houston. Right? Yet, she is able to do something with hers that I will never be able to do with mine. That is make people happy when she throws them into gear and sings. I, on the other hand, make large dogs roll over dead, small children run for cover and old men drop their few remaining teeth when I engage those same parts. In the same tradition, I have feet. Martha Graham had feet. Yet her feet went in all the right directions. It uses up half my brain capacity (which is a pitifully small base from which to start anyway) just to concentrate on all of that confusing "left, right, left, right, left..." stuff. So while we all may have the same parts (more or less) we all don't use them to perfection. I have no business singing on Broadway, I also have no business having children.

Some people get insanely huffy at that statement. They act like it is a sin to admit you have as much talent for being a parent as Roseanne does for belting out the "National Anthem". Being a parent (and no, I will not say "parenting" — I do my best not to "ing" if I can at all help it) is a pretty sensitive area. Yet, the same reaction does not come down on a person who announces they don't want to be an electromagnetic rocket engineer or some such thing.

Just say you don't want to have children and mouths drop, heads turn and the "twitters" and the "tsks" start.

One of my greatest detractors, a woman so horrified by my statement that she must shake her head violently and for all the world to see when the topic pops up, waited ten years to give birth. During that time she went through every horrid test and procedure to get pregnant that medical science can inflict on a person. Amazingly, now that she finally has the kids, she spends her days telling them how much they cut into her lifestyle — which pretty much consists of watching the soaps and the occasional Leeza. Why did she bother? She should have used those ten years learning corn farming. At least she would have been able to save on bundle on the popcorn she consumes between "General Hospital" and the "Young and the Restless".

She tells me that she had kids because she always wanted a home and family. Methinks her programming is a little short circuited. She likes the idea of having children. Worse yet, I think she likes the social acceptability that goes with that task. Beyond that, it is something to do when the hemorrhoid commercials come on. I wonder how long it takes a kid considered less important than "a very special edition" of Sally Jesse — "The Reunion of Sisters Who Drove A Stake in Each Other's Ears", to get a little jaded about life.

After the tsking dies down, I get barraged with all the reasons I must run out and grab the nearest Y chromosome-bearing creature and go at it under a bench. The first, and most laughable is, "Wouldn't you want a miniature you running around?" Who in the name of God needs another me walking this diseased and beaten Earth? You have got to be some kind of vain to think that you will be doing Mankind a great service to produce another as mutated as yourself. What two better qualities should someone who must devote hours generously molding an impressionable human form possess then vanity and self-centeredness?

The second reason I am given is that we all need someone to take care of us in our old age. First, that assumes that we are going to make it to whatever passes for old age these days. I mean, wouldn't it be really, really cruel if you gave up years of your life raising these kids for the sole purpose of having comfort in your old age and then got mowed down by a kamikaze bicycle messenger at fifty? Even if the messenger misses you and you make it to ninety or so, what are the odds that your offspring will be decent humans?

We all know exceptionally sweet people, truly terrific parents who, through no fault of their own, just spawn pond scum. I read that Hitler's mother was someone you wouldn't mind having over for tea and cookies to watch "Lifestyle of the Rich and Famous". You can raise them but you can't assure that they won't leave you on the sidewalk with a tin cup and a monkey when you hit eighty.

One of my all time favorite reasons for procreation is that it is a chance to do something important. After all, what could be more important than giving life? For goodness sakes, if you are the type of imbecile who forces another to undergo the horror that is childhood just so you can pat yourself on the back and say, "lookie here what I did", then that sort of proves you should keep your genes to yourself. Adopt an abused dog, clean up a polluted beach, throw a tomato at Geraldo Rivera — if you put your mind to it you can do lots of important things that have just as much of an impact on humanity.

Here's another one on my hit parade of dumb reasons to give birth. "I want to have something of my very own." Now that is real stability in action. If you are in that desperate need for a faithful possession, buy a cactus and name it Fred. It won't get all huffy if you get wrapped up in yourself and forget to feed it for a few weeks and it sounds like you probably will.

The old "everyone else has children," is a great excuse for people who, if their kid torched the bird house because all the kids were into destroying small forms of life this semester, would give the old, "If they jumped off the bridge would you follow blindly" speech.

I have a certain affinity for the "I wanted to see what it feels like" excuse. Wait a few years for some computer programmer to come up with a virtual birth software package. You can experience all the pain and sweating and still not inflict lifelong torture on some innocent creature. Besides, you may have always wondered what it was like to perform brain surgery but you don't tackle the guy seated next to you in the subway with a hacksaw just to indulge yourself in the experience. (Although there have been scattered reports of just that thing happening in certain sections of New York. However, in most civilized places this type of thing doesn't occur.)

Then there are people who must have been play-challenged in their own childhood because all they can talk about is how they want a cute little girl to dress up in frilly dresses or a little boy to deck out in sailor suits. I beg these people to get themselves a Barbie and Ken set. They will have hours of dress up fun ahead of them and Barbie and Ken are potty trained already.

One of the most laughable — and again vain — reasons for giving birth is, "I wanted to be immortal." So you think when your grandkid lands on Mars you are going to be there too? Wrong, you are going to be plant food then no matter how much you delude yourself. If you are someone who does or says anything even remotely useful while marking up the planet, chances are someone will remember you. Then again, if you are giving birth just so you can be remembered, you are probably too self centered to come up with some action that will provide wisdom and comfort for your fellow Man. In either case, please stop your gene pool where it rests.

Now here is the key to the Porte Think Before You Procreate System.

Just analyze the type of person you are and see if you have the qualities needed to make a decent parent. If you are like me and all of your plants are silk, and all your animals stuffed, yet you still think you will be a great parent. Think! Then rent a teething, untrained puppy. If you haven't stuffed it in the trash compactor within two weeks, you may have a shot at this parent deal someday.

If you love risk taking in areas you can control and want to reproduce just for the challenge of it all, yet, your usual reaction when life screws up your plans for the weekend by throwing a snow storm in your path is to scream until you are crimson all over — Think! Trust me folks, compete in a camel race across Morocco, swim the channel, take over a few businesses and merge some people out of a job but don't, don't, don't take on a task that requires real courage to face the unknown.

Before you decide to give birth — Think!

There is only one good reason for having a child. I will give you a few seconds to think of the answer...time's up! It is because you want to spend a huge hunk of the next several decades loving, encouraging (that's a big one), caring for, worrying over (there is lots of that), protecting and guiding a small, beautiful hunk of clay that is going to teach you more than you ever thought you could learn. Now wait, you have to do some more thinking. You need love, patience, foresight, patience, kindness, patience and oh yes, patience.

Hold it! Think some more! Why do you want to do this? The only correct answer is because you are basically a selfless person who will take joy in the wonderment that comes with forming the mind and soul of another human. You have to be willing to accept a life long commitment to the hardest job ever invented.

See, it really has nothing to do with you or your neurosis after all. Think about it.

Actually, I am getting better at this and I really think I will be a halfway decent mother when I hit about fifty. For some reason, Nature develops our bodies before our brains so when we have the wisdom to procreate, most don't have the ability or the energy. If Nature, which they say is perfect, screwed up like that, then how can humans shoulder the blame for giving birth for the wrong reasons. See, it isn't our fault we can't help it, we are victims of circumstance, it's beyond our control! Oops, maybe I was wrong — maybe I won't be ready for this parent thing until I'm fifty-five or sixty. Gee, if I wait that long, I hope my kid will be old enough to take care of me when I get really ancient.

13

Karmic Revenge

the delicate art of living in a family

⌒

If you are lucky — really, really lucky — you will love and hate the various and sundry members of your immediate family with equal passion for equal portions of your life. That's it. That's the best that it gets. Family is a lot like life itself. Regardless of whether the needle is pointing to loving it or hating it at any particular moment, at all times the thought — can't someone cook up a better alternative to all this nonsense — chews at your vital nerve endings. My friend Eileen, calling upon her vast knowledge of astrology and reincarnation, informed me that we are given specific family members to work out karmic debt from previous existences and to expand our souls. Well, there HAD to be a pretty big reason for all that trouble and there it is — karmic revenge.

You don't have to have Joan Crawford as a mother to feel the pressures of family life. Even if you got dealt a pretty decent hand, you soon learn that family dynamics resemble all too closely those of grade school — about third grade, fifth if you are fortunate. You have your requisite "cliques", finger pointing and constant chants of "teacher (replace with mom or dad) likes me better". As in any classroom, families come complete with your unabashed brown noses; kids totally baffled by the whole experience who sit in the corner occupied with something more fascinating and simple, such as their noses; the rebel drop outs and those of us swept along by the ugly tide. Grade school was agony unequalled by any other torture yet visited upon my soul (except for that blind date with the man who modeled every facet of his life after his idol, the one and only Junior Samples). Recalling those terrors of my youth, I have mapped out a plan for you to surf as painlessly as possible through family life without dooming yourself further to a worse Hell the next time around. Unless you are still twiddling with your nose, these few simple steps should be of vital assistance as you deal with your karmic retribution.

First, if you are a relatively decent adult who does their best to help out whenever possible and fulfil basic human familial requirements, remove all semblance of guilt from your thought processes. This is tough because every family has at least one or two guilt mongers who spew shame along your path hoping that it trips you up. They are usually the ones in most favor with the moms, dads, rich old aunts and uncles. Everyone loves them because they have never done anything...at any time in any way...to strive for, seek, grasp for any goal other than martyrdom. They hide their lack of aspirations by selling everyone on the theory that they gave it all up to be there ALWAYS in times of utmost crises, such as when Aunt Tilly's cat needs an emergency hair ballectomey.

When they are regaling you on their latest feat of humanity, guilt mongers will always pause — like a bad comic waiting for the requisite sympathy chuckle — for you to say either "Oh wow, you did all that?" or "You poor thing how do you do it all" before sighing and saying "Well, somebody has to do it...looks like it is always me." Then they will go on simultaneously polishing their mom's silverware and checking Uncle Irvin for gall stones.

If one of these brown nosers inhabits your family circle forget trying to show their true stripes to the old folks or plead your case about how much you do in your own quiet way. That's a backfire in the making and will doom you to hours of, "At least someone would care if I fell off the rocking chair because if it were up to you, they'd find me blue and hard on the floor two weeks after the fatal stroke" stories. Every good deed you do pales in comparison to theirs, so forget it. Your only consolation is that they have no life.

Of course, you could zing them occasionally by gathering up the old folks for a trip to Hawaii just as the guilt monger is slogging up the mountain in a blizzard hauling a sled stuffed with newly darned long johns and two months provisions by their teeth. However, Eileen warns that may have karmic repercussions and they might be twins next time! For the most part, silence is the best remedy. Eventually, they will fall asleep while cleaning Uncle Pete's cobra pit after an all nighter lubing Grandpa's Jag. and solve the problem for you. Yes, God does work in mysterious ways.

Second rule, don't take sides — don't associate with any "clique" that develops — and believe me, they will develop. I know of one family that fights from Halloween to Groundhog Day over their yearly Christmas party. No one wants to go and the battle realigns the balances of power and alliances until the next soiree but they have to show the world the depths of their holiday love and commitment no matter how many heads get shoved into the poinsettia punch during the planning of the darn thing.

The problem is made worse when members of each alliance "rat" on their current opponents. For instance, Aunt Bertha tells Uncle Ned that Cousin Wilma still sleeps with her anatomically correct Ken doll. Next year, however, Bertha and Wilma find themselves aligned together against Ned who has decided to invite eight not so tiny strippers in reindeer costumes to the big event. In a fruit cake induced craze, Ned finks to Wilma about what Bertha said the year before and another level of ground skirmishes erupt again.

No matter what, be Switzerland. Even the rebel drop has some redeeming qualities (unless they are a heroin shooting pimp or television evangelist) and usually rather sobering viewpoints with which you will find yourself in agreement. Besides, if you stay neutral you will get to hear all the rumors and gossip about everyone instead of just one side of the story all the time. Who could ask for more?

Finally, and most importantly, hang onto those traditions that make you flash back on the kitchen on a snowy afternoon when all the kids were piling in after sled riding, but don't become trapped by them. If you find yourself collapsing in a frazzled, exhausted heap in the corner exactly twenty-two hours after every holiday celebration, this is a symptom of two things. One, you are taking this family responsibility thing a wee too far and may need some serious psychological counseling or a trip alone to the Himalayas for a year or two. Two, you are probably one of the many people swept along in the great of tide of familydom. Like the crowd at K Mart's Dollar Days, a family can become too powerful and just crush your personality under its collective size 9 wides as it tramples on. Sure you may enjoy the memories brought about by a whipping up a good batch of Aunt Jeana's Ten Hour Baked Pelican Snout Souffle with the rest of them but try introducing your own microwavable delicacy on Christmas morning. After all, as we all know, a stagnant family is a dull family. There is no better way to get yourself known than to inflict some new concoctions on the clan every chance you can get. Soon you will either be known as the great chef of the family or the crazy relation trying to kill everyone off. Either way, it is better than being anonymous.

Just remember that, no matter what happens, take it with a ton or two of salt. Stand back, laugh and don't take it all too seriously.

Remember, according to Eileen, everyone is tossed together to be learning and improving with each step, not getting all goofy every time some pointy nose cousin three times removed snubs you. If you are not careful you could come back next time in a much more screwed up familial situation — you could be Benedict Arnold the 50th or worse — a Jackson or — the powers of the universe forbid — a Windsor.

14

Deciding How To Spend the Next Sixty Odd Years in One Fun Filled Afternoon

the folly of career day

~

Back in the days when the Soviet Union was alive and kicking, the government decided on the careers of its citizens. For example, if a kid spent a suspicious amount of time enjoying quiet moments with chickens, he was destined to become a chicken plucker — or a daytime television talk show host. I felt very superior about our free society that forbids such barbarity until I read a poll showing that 70 percent of the American public hate their jobs. (I wonder if that includes people who take stupid polls?) Seventy percent! Even if the poll was remotely accurate, I don't think, that in his darkest hour, Thoreau could have imagined so many lives of quiet desperation roaming around out there. So much for superiority.

Our first big career move hits us at the ripe age of about sixteen when we must decide if we are going to proceed to college. Now I know that Mozart had composed about a billion sonatas by that age but most of us are still learning the fine art of detecting ear wax buildup. At sixteen, I wasn't sure if I was going to be a physical therapist, a missionary or a belly dancer. At sixteen, our concerns should center around sending pornographic notes to the hunk in Algebra. (Actually, we should have our eye on the quiet, goofy kid in the corner because odds are he is going to be a zillionaire and the hunk a burnt out, obese drunk by forty. That alone proves how off our judgement is at sixteen.)

If we do go to college, we have to pick a major at twenty thus solidifying the next forty odd years of life unless we have parents who enjoy paying for our ever changing majors. However, it isn't a pretty sight to see a graduate hobble down the aisle planting toothless kisses on well wishers.

If we reject college (or it us), doom comes more quickly because our career choices center on jobs that provide little more than "security" — unless, of course, the company folds in fifteen years and the boss races off to Argentina with our pension. Barring that occurrence, there is still a good chance that the boredom causes us to go so mad that we perch atop a water tower one morning with an Uzi firing aimlessly at all forms of life scurrying below.

With typical genius, the American education system does nothing to prepare us to handle all the freedom we have to choose our life paths. Oh yeah, we learn all about pie and how it tries to square with that darned elusive "r" and Heaven forbid we not spend hours getting intimate with a medicine ball but provide courses exploring the millions of different careers in the naked city? Never. I can remember being driven to the point of stabbing myself in the liver with a protractor during Geometry class but no one bothered to tell me oceanographers existed. I developed a tic in Home Economics trying to make a jumper (now there is something I do just every free second I can grab) but did I learn that people can make a living digging up old bones like the ones we found in the back yard when Dad put in a pool? I didn't even know how fascinating Art History is until my once dear and now long lost friend, George, begged me to take it as an elective in my senior year in college.

All we had — and unfortunately still have — to guide us is an aberration called "Career Day," one of the most sadistic creations since the spiked shoe and the root of most of our occupational evils. That is when a bunch of frustrated employees in jobs that we already know too much about, get to spend a day out of the office by stressing to a group of impressionable children a one sided view of the total joy of walking in their footsteps. For each sucker they line up, they get a bonus like another vacation day or a free trip to Lizard Land (rides included!) or some such garden spot. Who cares really as long as they are away from their desks! Not since Satan organized his band of fallen angels has some demonic mind devised a scheme to get so many innocents to sign a pact jeopardizing their long term security.

With not so fond memories of those afternoons spent on forced marches from table to table listening to enthusiastic sales pitches — "carbon paper sales — get in on the office supply for now and the future" — I recently decided to crash one at a local high school. My first stop was at the airline recruiting booth. I had waited a long time to seek revenge on the airline industry. The perky flight attendant who had been around the globe a few too many times had just given her "travel around the world for free" speech when I raised my hand. "What happens when you have worked for about twenty years and you are making too much money and the company wants to hire cheaper, younger, sexier flight attendants and they toss you out of your job?"

The smile twittered a little but the perk remained. "That sort of thing doesn't happen at OUR airline...experience is needed and looked upon with reverence."

"Then why aren't you flying any more? Was it a pay cut and this job or good bye for good for you?" That hit a nerve. The wish for my slow and painful death came across her face and for a brief second her smile turned slightly downward.

"Any other reasonable questions from STUDENTS?" she begged. I turned to the crowd of groggy students and was a little heartened that some were showing actual signs of brain wave activity. "Did you tell them that in most of the cities they will see nothing more than the inside of a hotel room at best, oh, and did you get to the part about how all that flying and time zone changes just messes up the body clock?"

"The world of travel holds a great many opportunities."

"Granted. It also has some ugly downsides. So why don't you present both?" Before she could respond I took my leave with a dramatic turn but not before whispering to one not so fine young cannibal with eyes not yet completely glazed over, "Ask her what happens when you are 40,000 feet over no where and have three kids heaving up dinner."

My job done there I wandered over to the oil company kiosk and immediately asked the Prince of Paunch manning the booth how many experienced executives were "downsized" without pensions or medical benefits after the last merger. "Most of our employees were given early retirement benefits," he muttered through bovine lips.

"And what is left after you subtract a 'most' — a couple thousand human beings? And what about that last oil spill...that dropped stock prices so low I hear there hasn't been a promotion in your company since 1990." I ducked just in time to prevent the plastic oil rig he heaved at me from piercing my larynx.

This is the way it went from booth to booth, me sort of acting like a beacon of light spreading a little honesty and the two sided approach to their happy, peppy speeches until security forces escorted out the uninvited unfriendly. I did get in a parting shot, however. Just as they tossed me out the door, with raised hands and sort of Norma Rae-ish ferocity I shouted out, "Students, students, hear me! Refuse to go on to the next table until they explain to you what it takes to be a Geologist! Performance Art! Don't move until they define and tell you how to learn about Performance Art! Unite! Unite!"

If you are young enough to still make a few life changes, do something wacky like take a course that you would never think you would enjoy (audit it if you are anal retentive about your average.) Who knows, you might become as fascinated by Buffalo Dancing of the Great Northwestern plans as I was with Music Appreciation. If you are beyond those formative years, instead of buying another round at the local pub in which to drown your sorrows, consider taking a few night courses or contact Sally Struthers for a work at home guide. You might just find that real calling. What's worse, a life full of antacids and endless hours of listening to "Piano Man" or giving it all up to make less money but enjoy complete satisfaction as a 'gaiter wrangler at Alligator Heaven?

Better yet, hire yourself out to busy parents as a professional career day heckler. Eventually, you might get some changes made but even if you don't, you will have lots of fun equalling the score for all of those lectures you had to sit through.

15

Turn Off the Voices in Your Mind

leave the folks at home when you go out in the world

~

History tells us that the voices in her head told Joan of Arc how to defeat her enemies in battle. Well, maybe that's true, but no matter who or what rattled on in her skull, I guarantee that she never had to contend with the likes of the voices of the few dozen relatives who cluttered up my brain waves for the first thirty-five years of my life. I should have learned a lesson from that other Joan and gotten rid of them earlier — after all, look where her voices landed her.

We all know people who can only get their jollies by kvetching about the actions of others that are out of their self-prescribed bounds of acceptability. To give you an idea of how stringent those confines can be, bringing the wrong kind of dessert to the Elks Harvest Moon covered dish dinner is considered way over the line and grounds for weeks of gossip in certain territories of my gene pool.

In fact, if the Barrymores produce more than the average share of distinguished actors, the Peales an abundance of great painters and the Kennedys ah...er statesmen...then my family is right up there by producing an Olympic amount of what I like to affectionately call Sideline Judgers.

Life is a tightrope and if your little toe goes off the edge a bit they are there like crocodiles in long aprons and black "nun shoes" waiting to snap off your legs. Having them in your head is worse than burning in an eternal Hell where you must listen to endless football half time shows at which Frank and Kathy Lee Gifford perform a musical rendition of their lives together. (Kathy plays the roles of both Cassidy and Cody.)

Their battle cry, "What will people think?" aims to strike terror in the hearts of the would be renegade. Personally, I hold out eternal hope that "people" are thinking about how we are going to give our children a future despite the huge debt we have so piggily amassed or how we are going to control genetic engineering before we all become pink eyed cyclops, but the Judgers think differently. If it is difficult for you to listen to Andy Rooney belly aching about soap containers or the size of ear wax removal syringes for a few minutes each week, try sitting around every Sunday and holiday with a bunch of people who whine about everything from people's love lives and career choices down to their kitchen color schemes. (Auntie Nilda is particularly harsh on avocado green, by the way.)

When Mrs. Johanson down the street remarried just one year after her husband took leave of his earthly body and she went off to live with her new mate in Greece, she provided fodder for the gab mill from Thanksgiving straight up until New Year's Eve. That's when they learned that Mr. Anthony sold his drugstore and moved to a cabin in Montana accompanied only by a copy of "Walden" and a pet squirrel he christened "Buddy". That episode carried them well into Easter when the topic switched to "How could Jacqueline Onassis be such a good mother when her daughter ACTUALLY lived with her husband prior to wedlock?" (And you thought only the crew of the Enterprise got trapped in time warps.)

Some people just sluff these types off and go on their merry ways...others of us — for reasons medical science may never deduce — pack them up in our cerebellum and bring them along wherever we may roam. For years, I had the whole knitting circle imbedded somewhere over my right occipital lobe monitoring and commenting on everything I did or planned to do. If I wanted to splurge on a vacation, I could hear Auntie Theresa yapping about how wasteful I was and how little I cared about preserving money for the disaster she just knew would befall me. After all, what is life if not a constant preparation for some horror that is destined to slam down and crush us all? If I wanted to go away for the weekend with a guy, Cousin Anna was in my ear snipping away about my loose morals. Her children would never do such a thing. Of course, until they were thirty, her kids were afraid to answer the phone because she convinced them that every person on the other side was the killer she warned them about constantly since she strapped them down in their protectively padded play pens. I swear I could even hear her simultaneously sucking on her fifteenth chocolate bon bon as she pontificated. That's how vivid these voices were. Even though I lived five hundred miles away, they were there every second of the day...commenting, criticizing, judging (and reminding me to dust the top of my picture frames.)

One day it almost brought me to the breaking point. I was trying to decide if I should buy some out of state property. First, Theresa's voice piped up — "You were a scaredy-cat as a kid, the first sign of trouble, you will be running home."

Anna gobbled down another bon bon — "What the heck you are trying to prove now? You think you are better than everyone already," she slurped.

"You will never see your family again. You are rejecting your parents." That was Uncle Alberto — another harbinger of lunacy.

The voices grew louder and louder even though I put the radio on the "All Obnoxiously Loud Rock Music All The Time" station, found one of the fifty television stations featuring the "All in the Family — The Loud Years" marathon and karaoked with Patty Le Belle.

"Why can't you be like everyone else?" "Your too good for everything we have?" "Why do you always want to be different?" I knew these thoughts were insane but I couldn't stop them. I shut my eyes and could see them cleaning string beans on the back porch comparing horror stories of family members gone awry. The din grew louder. The room began to spin and then — in a blinding whirl — everything went black.

I don't know how long I was in the dark but eventually I saw a bright light in the distance. It continued to glow and come closer until it seemed near enough for me to touch. As my eyes adjusted, I could see that atop the beam was a small asexual, elfin figure. I was not afraid of the creature. After all, it was not wearing a house dress or smoking a small, green rope cigar AND it couldn't speak. It held out a radiant hand and as I grabbed it we began swishing past the space-time continuum. Before I knew what hit me, I found myself looking down into the homes of some of the people who were always cluttering up my head.

We hovered above Uncle Paulo's and Aunt Josephina's home first and then descended into it, slipping right through the ceiling and walls. The elfin spirit actually tried to have us land on the sofa since we were now invisible but we kept slipping off the plastic covers. We settled for a seat on the velvet rendering of Sinatra on stage in Vegas.

They sat in stony silence. That alone startled me because when they are in a crowd these two never stop flapping their gums. They crave an audience more than Newt Gingrich. Paulo sat dusting his trombone...actually, it looked as though he were almost stroking it but I would rather not think about him stroking anything so I convinced myself it was just a real careful polishing. It came to me that I remembered hearing stories about how he used to play trombone in a band as a kid but gave it up when everyone told him it was time to get a "real" job. He has been hauling fish at the docks for the past thirty years and judging from the number of nights he spends getting totally plastered in the local bar, I have a sneaky suspicion that it is not as spiritually and emotionally fulfilling to him as was playing his music.

Come to think of it, I don't think fish hauling gives him the opportunity to find the physical fulfillment he craves either. However, that brings me back to his fondness for that trombone and...well let us just go on...shall we?

My aunt looked like I had never seen her...solemn and sunken. It is amazing how your facial features change when you aren't screeching. She slammed the lid on the pot of spaghetti sauce and grabbed the curtains with an eye pasted onto some small, forlorn hole trying to make a home there. She immediately snuffed the life out of it with a handy needle and thread and a pretty dexterous pair of hands. I suddenly remembered hearing stories about the job offer she received to work at one of the largest designer houses in New York when she was only seventeen. She had the talent but just couldn't muster the courage to venture into the "evil" city every day so she worked at the switch-board of the local office of "The Really Pu-trid Fabric-O-Rama" (this is even before they went nationwide!) before marrying Paulo. He had proposed to her in a drunken stupor after three overtime shifts towing shrimp and before he could sober up, he had sealed his doom.

Dinner continued in silence. They were like robots, performing tasks that required no thought or caring. They had done this so many times before. In fact, I realized that every time I went into their house, they were doing just what they were doing now! It sud-denly hit me that nothing about them ever changed (except the length of their mus-taches.) Their lives didn't have phases — they were the original flatliners.

The spirit signaled me and we were off again. I soon found myself sliding around on top of the plastic furniture coverings of Cousin Marina's house that she shared with her husband, Rocco. They were the ones who put a halt to their daughter attending col-lege in upstate New York because, as they said right in front of her to half the free world, "We would never trust her alone out in society."

The house was quiet except for the tele-vision they had tuned to the Movie Chan-nel. I knew Marina was a movie freak. What

I didn't know was that she kept stacks and stacks of books and magazines on every movie star since Chaplin in closets all around the house. After calling Rocco, "You good for nothing idiot" for the third time in a row she ran into her sewing room. Instead of sewing, however, she began to act out scenes from the great old flicks in front of a big standing mirror. I felt more than a little uneasy watching her try out her most seductive moods on the full length mirror and flip her hair around, especially since it had more waxy buildup than her front foyer. At least it solved the riddle of why someone who dedicated a whole room to sewing would always say, "Are we having turkey?" when someone mentioned baste stitches.

Suddenly, my eyes were opened, really opened, for the first time in my life. What did I care what these people said about me? They would make the audience of a Jerry Springer show look well adjusted. Instead of fear, I should only be giving them pity (and a life time supply of plastic cleaner.) Here I had spent years letting people who messed up their lives, dictate mine. I was free! I was liberated! I was a new woman! I was sure my life would now be my own! I was falling off the plastic. In the nick of time, the spirit grabbed me, guided me back to my home and disappeared.

So did the voices in my head. Now, when I sit through holiday meals I don't boil in anger at their intolerance. I don't even get angry when Theresa reminds everyone that HER daughter lives right next door to her and would never think of even reading a book about "abnormal things" such as holistic healing.

When I make a decision I don't try to envision what they would say about it and factor that into the process. Those days are gone. The only voice I listen to now is the one that comes from deep within my guts. I don't know why I hadn't paid attention to that one years before. Unlike Auntie Theresa, it always sends out encouraging and wise signals. Besides, unlike her, it never once steered me wrong about a sale at Bloomingdales.

16

It Doesn't Always Pay To be Nice To Men... Or Women

dating made simple

I have a funny little quirk. (Actually, I have several but for the sake of brevity let's concentrate on one, OK?) If I am going to expend energy in a relationship with a male of the species then I am going to be nice to the guy. Were I trapped for ten years on an Aleutian isle with a band of escaped ax murderers, I might not feel the need to act all cuddly and confectionery to my companions. When I choose to erase some of my hours with another human being, however, that's a different story. Many militant female friends have accused me of being a marshmallow but I figure too much of life is a battle with people you don't really want to be around, so why fight with a housemate? If you can't stand the guy enough to be civil to him, buy a dog to help you through those lonely hours. Relationships are hard work, at best. What's the point of looking for more trouble?

Some people never have to worry about those "dog lonely moments", however. These are the inhabitants of an odd subculture who enjoy making the lives of their "loved ones" a level of Hell even Dante couldn't imagine. This goes beyond being a little pushy or demanding or cranky or bossy or any of those foibles one can live with aided only by a small glass of wine. This is a sicko need to make their loved ones the recipients of the outpourings of their every neurosis and insecurity. The goofy part is that these people are always in a relationship! Women, forget all of those "Snag That Man By Changing Your Eyes to His Favorite Color with Contacts" articles. Men, put sensitivity training aside. PLEASE! If you want to be with someone desperately, one quick way is through the door of downright snottiness.

I had a ringside view of this type of relationship years ago courtesy of one of my roommates. She and her boyfriend had come home early from dinner and she headed immediately for the bedroom. He preferred to see the rest of "Monday Night Football". After a few minutes, she came out regaled in her finest ankle length flannels (that will get those juices flowing). She interrupted Howard Cosell's rendition of the life story of the kicker's grandfather's struggle to leave Communist Poland by announcing, "I am going to bed now."

Well, what do you say to that? There are many variations on the theme, but we opted for the traditional. "Good night."

She came out a few minutes later. "I am going to bed now and I want you to come with me." Wow, talk about enticing your man into bed with hot talk!

"I will be there after the game." Good, two points for him. I thought I saw the makings of a spine. Out of her cage again she stomped, with a determined look in her eye, and the will to win. After all, this was the guy who she sent scurrying around to three different Mexican restaurants in a blinding snow storm until he found one that had the perfect amount of cilantro in their salsa.

"I am going to bed now and I don't want you waking me up when you come in so come to bed now!" That pseudo spine dissolved into a yellow streak. He quietly shuffled into the bedroom missing both an eighty yard Namath pass and his chance to step into human-hood. I could just hear Howard doing the narration on that one. "And there he goes, head down, tail sagging...and what a majestic tail it could be if only he knew how to hold his own against the mighty force of the flannel beast. Rounding the corner for the bedroom he looks as though he might balk...but no...it was just a momentary bout with noxious, vicious stomach acid. A sad, sad day for manhood ladies and gentlemen — a sad day indeed."

Maybe it is my lot to interact with several — shall we say — forceful women. I shared an apartment briefly with one who came to Washington to marry a guy she had met while she was a summer intern. Since she absolutely refused to live with him prior to the big night (but felt no qualms about the two of them having the sex life of a hare as long as she was home when the sun came up — I call it the vampire sex fixation), I opened my big mouth and said she could share my studio apartment for a few months. Life was relatively normal between us — but oh what she didn't do to that poor man.

A few weeks before their marriage, he decided to go off to his doom with a gathering of about five friends from the old office. The party was at my place since he lived in a group home that had the ambiance — and smell — just slightly less appealing that the gorilla's pen at the National Zoo. Everything went along fine until around ten when Miss. Cheery Pants stood up and announced that it was, "Time for all of your friends to depart because I have to get up and work with numbers in the morning." I started to make a case for her stretching out in the dressing room on a few overcoats but the poor old groom-to-be hurried everyone out the door and down to the Hawk and Dove for the remainder of the celebration. I don't know whatever happened to them but I do know that they both wore white to the wedding and several people questioned which one was the bride.

This is not to say that I completely fault these women. Sometimes I wish I had that gene that would make me less accommodating to men. I have learned the hard way that it really doesn't always pay to be nice to them — it seems to upset the balance of their Y chromosome. One of my first big loves was a man for whom I would have done anything. We are not talking scaling mountains and robbing banks or worse here, folks — nothing psychotic. I just figured the best way to keep him was to be totally agreeable and not ruffle the waters. It didn't help matters that I thought it was just great that he wasn't one of those "let's spend every breathing second together types."

So darned amiable was I that he didn't think I would mind a bit about his "real" girlfriend. I discovered her existence when her picture fell out of his wallet and he replied to my query, "Oh that is my real honey.. my special girl." I later found out the skunk had a little harem of fools like myself whom he occupied his time with when he couldn't be with her. So much for agreeability.

Maybe I was being too harsh on my old roommates.

Another time being too compliant got me in trouble was when I dated a guy who thought that I wouldn't mind if he used my house, my food, my energy and time and my entertaining skills to promote his career and then left me behind to marry another woman. When he finally got that promotion that enabled him to keep one of us in the manner we had always expected to live, it was "adios" to me. He never really gave me a reason for choosing her over me except that he said she understood him more. I understood him a little too late — he was a manipulating, evil, two headed worm. (Good thing that it is against my better nature to hold a grudge.) It didn't escape my notice that he, like the snake before him, had a bevy of women from which to choose.

Yes, I WAS being too harsh on my old roommates. Go sisters, go. Avenge the rest of us!

Tired of being the "hurtee", I tried to change my ways. With the next guy I dated I set the ground rules right from the beginning.

When he asked where I wanted to go for dinner, I stopped myself from saying, "Ah, I'll eat anything but turnips and eel fritters — whatever." "I'll only eat Italian tonight — Northern Italian and I want a place that has the best carbonara," was my clipped response.

I held my breath for a minute and realized how much I didn't like me. "OK fine, I'll look for one. Should I pick you up at six or seven?" He was getting into this!

"Seven, of course, I need time to prepare."

"Of course, how silly of me. I am sorry. Seven it is."

The whole evening went on with this nauseating pace. By the time I demanded that he retrieve the car from a half block away so I wouldn't have to walk too far from the restaurant, I had him hooked. When I insisted that he bring me home instead of going to the movie because the flame from the cherries jubilee, "Caused a migraine that will just be intolerable," he was way, way too eager to comply. He babbled on like a puppy on black beauties about what an enriching experience that night had been for him. I wanted to run myself through on the umbrella stand as soon as I walked in the door but apparently I had given him a night to remember.

This went on for three more dates. At one point I demanded that we leave the Japanese steak house because that, "Awful smoke is just destroying my hair." He was out of there in a flash as though the chef on the next table had let loose with the machete that found a home in his posterior.

I couldn't take it anymore. As he was simultaneously driving and waving a napkin at my head trying to desmoke me...I shouted out. "What in the world is wrong with you?"

"I am sorry, am I causing you a draft?"

I realized that this was going to require more drastic action. We had an ice skating date that Saturday afternoon. It was, of course, my idea to skate. When we got to the rink, we met some of his friends. This was my opportunity to move into nag overdrive. As soon as we met up with his buddies, I refused to go on the ice. "I don't wish to skate. It is an absurd activity that fills the time of the middle class. I do not wish to partake."

At first he was going to skate with his friends anyway but then he couldn't "Just watch me sit there so alone." Was this guy a case or what? Even in my most agreeable younger days I never was this big a doormat. At least I hoped I wasn't. Nah, even I wasn't this bad. Was I? We left the rink promptly.

One the way home I finally expected the explosion.

"You know what?"

This was going to be it.

"What?" I replied with a note of anticipation.

"You are really nice. You are a sweet lady."

I grabbed the steering wheel and pulled us over to the side. "What the heck is wrong with you?"

Was I driving too quickly? I'm sorry..."

"NO! And stop acting like a darned slave!"

"I'm sorry, what do you want me to do?"

"Watch a Bogart Marathon and take massive notes. Right now, I'll just settle for some signs of life."

"I'm sorry, I thought I was making you happy."

Hours of discussion later that night (halted only by his incessant jumping up and down to bring me more coffee and fluff the sofa pillows behind me) yielded the amazing fact that he felt my shenanigans were his avenue to "really express love and do something" for someone. The more I bitched the more wanted and less alone he felt.

I consulted a world renowned psychiatrist who explained it to me in simple terms. "There are lots of rats out there and too many people willing to accommodate them. The world is full of accommodators, you know. The chances of finding someone who is neither a doormat or complete bully is pretty iffy at best. If you want happiness, buy a parakeet but it will probably die before you do. You will need extensive counseling in either case. Here's my card."

Using that valuable advice I have formulated my own theory on relationships. There are probably a good number of relatively healthy ones out there but if you are one of those people who want a relationship — I mean, if you really, really hate to be alone at all costs — and can stand yourself while you do it — become a beast. I guarantee you will be with someone immediately.

Or try to adopt my theory of life. That regardless of what it does to your love life, it is better if the person you have to be with every day — yourself — doesn't make you retch on sight, and maybe you should get that parakeet after all...better yet a tortoise. Odds are it will outlive you.

17

Did I Ever Tell You You're Not Really My Hero?

hero worship takes all the fun out of staring in the mirror

～

I spent a good portion of my cavity prone impressionable years dreaming that I was any and every perfect woman who had ever lived — in short, almost any woman who wasn't me. Monday, I was Amelia Earhart, Tuesday, Eleanor Roosevelt, Wednesday, Queen Guinevere and Thursday (in addition to being Prince spaghetti day) was always pioneer day. That's when the school bus magically transformed into a covered wagon; the crowded suburban tract houses into tall Western mountains dotted with wild animals, ticked off Indians (I'm sorry, this was pre-political correctness) and other terrors so horrid they would make the strong, independent women of today quake in their Donna Karan stockings.

After the first landing on the Moon, I was Mrs. Neil Armstrong for almost a full month. This was also pre-liberation. Besides, it was enough of a stretch just to imagine that a hero as perfect as an astronaut would pick a kid with braces and knock knees as a wife — forget being one! Even my imagination couldn't take that giant a leap.

Still, since I was never what you would call a good sleeper — or even a moderately decent sleeper or even a half-way decent sleeper — I would spend hours under the covers pretending my bed was a boat skimming the waters of the Mekong Delta like that of the female war photographer I had read about, or the carriage that carried Dolley Madison from the White House as she escaped the British with a picture of George Washington tucked safely away in her corset. Even if I could never be as good as them, I could dream. Between the hours of ten in the evening and one in the morning or whenever I finally gave into the human frailty of sleep — something I am sure never hampered Clara Barton or Annie Oakley, I became a vicarious hero. Tucked into my warm bed, safe in the walls of my home, with nothing around I could fall over, I could at least taste that feeling of being perfect.

I also killed many a heinously boring school hour (but no matter how many I exterminated, more kept coming at me, I am sorry to report) healing people like Madame Curie did or conquering France like Joan of Arc; who, after many battles with Sister Barnabas, I was finally able to take as my patron saint. (The good sister insisted that I chose John the Baptist since I was named after my father but there was no way I was going to follow the steps of a man who ate locusts and stomped around the desert for months on end in a hair suit. I itched for weeks when my mother put too much starch in my uniform. Besides, I didn't even like to spending more than a week in Atlantic City digging sand out of my bathing suit and eating cotton candy. He might have been a hero too but enough was enough.)

I was a regular Walter Mitty morphing myself into these heroic woman who apparently got at birth higher than average brain power, steady nerves, straight spines, clear eyes, and zitless faces. They guffawed at self doubt, never knew what it was like to feel directionless, and certainly never lost their temper. They never said the wrong thing, like asking a woman whose husband ran off with the town tramp if life was treating her OK lately. They never did the wrong thing, like choke on air and make a hacking, wheezing scene just when the toast was given at a wedding. These people were perfection in skin.

After all, they were all heroes — born to be something I just knew I could never be. I figured they got an extra blast of gene purifying rays on the production line because they were like no woman who ever crossed my path. Who, by the way, pretty much consisted of females under five feet tall, with distressfully large thighs who dressed in black and moaned "Oh, God love you darling. You just don't want to know how much I am suffering in pain today. Sit down and let me tell you."

The roots of my little, weird world were not only in my little, weird mind. It was all the rage in those days for books and newspapers to make everyone who did even just one semi-decent thing some kind of saint in BVD's. Climb a mountain — you are a hero. Get elected to office — you are a hero. Sing a good song — you guessed, you are a hero. (And they said we teenagers lacked self control.)

The schools contributed to this madness. They couldn't (and still can't) teach Math or History worth a darn. They didn't bother sharing Shakespeare or Homer with us but they could create heroes at a drop of a hat. Although they also kept pounding into our heads how frail and fallible most mortal creatures be, teachers insisted on making "Heroes 101" a required course for all children in this pre Tabloid Journalism era. It was sort of like — "We know you don't stand a snowballs chance of polishing his shoes. You will never be as honest as Abe or brave and wise as George or as brilliant as Thomas, or versatile as Ben but make sure you know how much better than you they were." Way to bolster those young minds, don't you think?

It was no use trying to aspire to be like these idols. Forget that. I didn't master the intricate art of shoe lace tieing until third grade, how could I think of setting off to cross the Arctic or climb Mount Everest? If I learned nothing else, I learned that some of us just have it and some of us don't. I could only take some meager satisfaction in the assurance the human beast came in such higher forms.

Just when I resigned myself to the genetic doom of this non-heroic existence, a new and completely different trend in historical revisionism was born. It started in the mid-'70s and was given the official title of "Rip The Moral Stuffing Out Of Any Creature Who Dares To Make A Name For Him/Herself." Those who know these things (and tell all the rest of us how much they know about

155

these things) tell us that the era was ushered in by the fall of the House of Nixon. This is when we learned that not only did the Emperor not have any clothes but he couldn't even buy a good pancake makeup to keep the sweat off his upper lip.

There was so much fun in exposing Nixon's many errors, they just couldn't stop. Hero building is not nearly as much fun as crushing out their guts. Face it, we would rather play Doom than interact with a CD-Rom explaining the values and importance of Etruscan Art.

It's that old theory; if bad news sells better than good, then really gross stuff about people we are jealous of, will go off the charts. As usual, the old theory works like a charm. (And is, by the way, one of the secrets of Howard Stern's, Rush Limbaugh's and that paragon of positivity, Pat Buchanan's success.)

Now, instead of filling pages with only the good aspects of a person's personality, we went out of our way to bring every public figure down to the level of octopus droppings. No one was safe.

- Abraham Lincoln — formerly known as sole saver or the Union, freer of slaves — a man who walked miles barefoot over cow drop laden plains to return a book, was now a lunatical manic depressive who disregarded civil liberties, was majorly whipped and had some serious constipation problems. (The latest dish is that he could play the lead in "The Birdcage" without having to act the part.)

- George Washington — formerly known as Father Of Our Country, first in war, first in peace and never first in line for the figgie pudding, was now that sterile dirty, old man rendered in that delicate state from a wicked case of syphilis that he may have contracted while horsing around with his best friend's wife.

- Thomas Jefferson — formerly known as brilliant writer, thinker, architect and farmer; was now just the father of Lord knows how many illegitimate children with his slave. Why talk about the making of the Constitution when we can talk about the making of Sally Hemmings?

- Amelia Earhart — formerly known as great courageous flyer; was now a hot head who went off on the flight ill prepared and undertrained.

Whether we want to or not, we now learn the intimate grotesque details of sex lives, hygiene habits and potty training of the rich and famous. It has become so bad that people can actually raise their public opinion levels by telling us how unheroic they are. Princess Diana, a woman never short on unheroic qualities, got a socko 75 percent approval rating after she went on the BBC and told the world (and her two small sons) that she was a suicidal, bulimic who hated her husband and was unfaithful in her marriage. Madonna gets more popular with every grab of her crotch, Michael Jackson with every new nose. Just think of what Jack the Ripper could have done with his self image if he were around now. Attila the Hun would make the cover of "Time" at least twice a year. I can just see it now, "'I can't stop plundering,' An Intimate Confession Of One Of Our Century's Most Successful Barbarians." We used to watch "Queen for A Day", now our daytime television screens show us "Slut for a Day".

So what is the result of this turn about? Instead of moaning that we can never be heroes, we average mortals now wail and gnash our teeth over the fact that there are no more heroes. We are exposing the bad side of everyone and showing them to have — oh no — human flaws! What will become of our children if they have no one to feel inferior to? (We are doing this at the same time we are telling kids to march to their own drummers and just "be the best you's you can be!" No wonder they are a little daffy.)

Call me wacky, but I have had my fill of this whole hero-antihero thing.

Hey, here is a unique idea! Let's save ourselves a lot of self loathing and our children
mass confusion and the cost of Xanax, by just
growing up and knocking off this need for
worship fixation. You can love Barbra
Streisand's voice and hate her politics. (The
same could be said about Sinatra but he
changes his so often depending on who will
invite him to the White House that I am
never sure whether I am for or against him.)

Similarly, just because someone has the
hormones to give mesmerizing theatrical
performances or make great speeches or hit
baseballs further than anyone else doesn't
mean he might not also have a basement full
of petrified bat wings that he visits only on
the full moon. One does not negate the
other...in fact, the more talented the person
the chances are the more bat wings he may
have in hiding. Buy their records, go to their
movies and just leave it at that. You don't
need to dress or walk or talk or eat or do
ANYTHING like that person and for goodness sakes don't dress your little girls in
ripped gloves and crosses because Madonna
wears them. Ah, don't let your little girls do
anything because Madonna does it.

Instead of making everyone the personi-
fication of pure good or pure evil, take the
good and the bad, add them up and come up
with a human. This keeps them down to

Earth and raises the rest of us above slug. Pick and choose — use a little discrimination. The next time you want to idolize someone just think of what you do when you see a great dress that happens to have those shoulder pads worthy of the front four of the 49ers. You buy the dress, rip out the shoulder pads and wear it, right? So, just picture your hero-in-the-making as a blue silk with a slit up the side but really cheesy looking buttons (guys, you can substitute a great tuxedo that comes with a dorky vest) and have your way with them. While you are at it, picture yourself as a stunning red Oscar de la Renta — you might start liking you a little more.

18

Laughing In The Face Of The Faceless

life among the bureaucrats

~

While I know it is a bit brazen to be so bold even in this shameless age, I must proudly proclaim that I am a card carrying rebel. No, I don't live on a farm in Woodstock and line my walls with old "flower power" signs. I just have a visceral reaction to the decrees of self proclaimed rulers. Government and corporate "authorities" have told me repeatedly that I can be quite the crimp in the colon. Even loving family members note that any provocation from imperious bureaucrats causes me to go into orbit. To these fine folks, friend and foe alike, I say a hearty, "Thank you very much, it's a gift."

From an early age I was incapable of keeping my mouth shut in the face of bullying — literally. That very poignant moment of realization came upon me in kindergarten. It was snack time in early spring. I was enjoying a well deserved respite after a particularly taxing jump rope competition. It was my first foray into the every girl for herself world of double dutch. Suddenly, out of the Playdough, came the pudgy hand of one Kevin Mahoney, alias the "Terrorist of Milk and Cookie Hour." For months he had struck fear in the hearts of all puny children in K1. Now my milk was a target of one of his commando raids. I had only seconds to protect my prized cache. I could have cried. I could have tattled. I could have acquiesced. Something inside me snapped, however, and my innate instincts boiled to the surface. I used the only weapon available. Kevin did not get my milk but he did wind up with an exquisite consolation prize: a semi-permanent imprint of my teeth imbedded deep into his porky paw. I realized then that I would be someone who, when attacked by the big bully, would always bite back.

Something else became obvious to me that fateful day. I discovered just how much society frowns upon such self preservation tactics. The teacher reprimanded me! The larcenist of table 3D wasn't even given one of her famous cross-eyed looks. Apparently, it was better to let him take a chunk out of my hide than be "anti-social." At that tender age, my life long quest to correct this basic injustice had begun.

That quirk in society that demands the acceptance of the tyranny of the brute reared its ugly head at another key moment during my vulnerable childhood. Several members of a local youth group were protesting the actions of one of our more overbearing adult overseers cursed with what had to be the worse case of prickly heat ever recorded. Having received no satisfaction from the board of directors, we planned a mass resignation for the next meeting. The aggrieved were to stride in single file, heads held high in indignation, plop our uniforms on the front desk and quit. In our minds, this would be the most inspiring procession since Patton paraded through Germany.

Plans hummed along until the night of the big meeting. At zero hour, my cohorts scattered like flies off the nose of a flu-ridden rhinoceros. There was just one scrawny kid stumbling up the aisle pulled by the weight of her braces. At least Patton always had his dog by his side.

When I was finally able to corner my fainthearted pals they confessed that they had received lectures from their parents about the evils of upsetting the status quo.

They all had reputations to worry about and couldn't have little Egbert making waves. After all, people would most assuredly talk if we upset a long established town institution. We couldn't have that. It was better to swallow injustice than tick off the elders. Again, I saw a pattern that remains unsettling. In the "land of the free and the home of the brave," we teach our children to yield to anything pretending to be an authority figure.

In a way, I understand how this fear has imbedded itself deep into our collective human brain. The world has always been a pretty spooky place. From the time we slithered out of primordial glop, Man has had to contend with dinosaurs, meteor showers and your occasional rampaging barbarian. Feudal lords, sadistic kings, ransacking armies and other legends in their own minds have conspired throughout History to turn the average person into a cowering wreck. Protection came in the security of groups such as families, towns and clubs. This need to huddle together in secure little clusters became ingrained. Too ingrained. Even as we evolve into a society with more individual freedom and power, we still crumble into blathering idiots every time a bully with a thyroid condition steps into our path.

Bureaucrats that suffered through hours of hideous potty training have replaced the beasts of yore. He may not have to worry about being the main course of a Tyrannosaurs, but a taxpayer is as fearful of a hungry, wild eyed, tromping tax assessor. She may not stay up nights dreading the invasion of a plundering band of savages but a small businesswoman will go gray and lose valuable bone building calcium worrying over the proper completion of pages of busywork designed by a government worker seeking revenge on the world for the prom night that never happened. As these creatures grow larger and more powerful (with our money might I add) they become like a modern day fire breathing dragon. The little person who dares spit in its beady eye becomes instant flambe'.

The dragon controls all aspects of our lives. The Federal and state governments are like Siamese octopuses pawing into every crevice of our lives. The friendly local grocery store is now part of a conglomerate that bubbles over with the warmth and compassion of Don Rickles during an attack of killer gas. Cable companies and studio executives dictate not only what we see but when we will see it. Grown people have to present a doctor's excuse to get a refund for a blasted airline ticket. Speaking of getting sick, we can't even do that without the express written consent of ten insurance companies. It is an often proven fact that as a nation we swallow more anger than Fishwich sandwiches. We take it when we have to stand on line at the motor vehicle department for so long that they deliver our birthday cakes there. We quietly build another room onto our business to accommodate the paperwork some bureaucratic wizard dreamed up after a romantic interlude with a bottle of Apricot Schnapps. We accept it when the Post Office misdirects Aunt Hildegard's Prune Wonders to an outpost in the Antarctic and charges us ten dollars to do the honor. We take it and we take it from the dragon.

Now I admit that the dragon is hard to fight because he is a lot like fast food. We know it will eventually make our arteries look like the San Diego Freeway at five PM but we also know that it is a lot easier to wolf down a "meat-o-cow" burger than figure out those silly fat, sodium and cholesterol charts. Not until they stretch us out like a carp in the coronary unit, do we realize that maybe we should not have taken the easy way out. The dragon chops away at our freedoms quietly like cholesterol does our arteries. It is as easy to ignore bloated bureaucratic bullies like we ignore the lard we are throwing past our lips. We are finally becoming alert to the horrors of fat. Now we just need to take it a step further and think of bureaucrats as big globs of blubber in suits and dresses.

So what should we do, you ask? It's easy. Pick out your favorite bureaucrat and turn the tables on them...find the one government program that really galls you and make a phone call — or send one fax or postcard a day to the media, the oversight committees — anybody who can help you. Or think of the insurance policy or airline rule that stick in your esophagus the most and once a day — every day — give it to them. Think of it like taking your vitamins only without the bitter after taste.

Oh, yes you do have time! There are commercials on television — you do sit on hold — you have a phone in your car — you have time. Just think of the therapy involved. Mad at your boss? Vent it at your bureaucrat. Your kid knocked over the Ming vase? Vent it at your bureaucrat. Hate your mother in law? Vent in on your pet bureaucrat. If you make time to pop a pill, have a drink, listen to a meditation tape or see a shrink, you can make time for one little note. Just keep repeating your own mantra — "I pay your salary, you worm. I pay your salary."

Don't delay — not only will you be doing something good for the future of your country (and deep down, don't you really want to tell your grandchildren you tried to give them something better?) but you will find an easy way to lower your blood pressure, relax you nerves and get a wonderful sense of power...There is only one other activity that promises those same results and I can guarantee that this won't get you (or anyone you know) pregnant.

19

What Martha Stewart Doesn't Tell You About Entertaining

forget polishing silver, make sure you have emergency food prepared

~

Much like childbirth, nothing can give you more momentary joy followed by agonizing pain that causes you to curse forever the moment of ecstasy that got you into the mess in the first place — like entertaining. If you live alone, the idea of cooking for a group of people can be a source of excitement. Actually, if you live alone, the idea of doing anything besides eating out of a take out bag while using the remote control to ring in to Alex ahead of the other three Jeopardy contestants, can be a thrill. You get that sudden flash of wonderment at the possibility of using your pots for something other than a home for wayward plants; that tingling sensation at the thought of actually setting a table and the shear giddiness of dreaming about your oven being more than a stashing place for your sister's cat when she needs a sitter on short notice. You pull out the old recipe books, make shopping lists and let the imagination run wild.

Forget what all of those "women's magazines" tell you. It is not as much fun to cook for yourself as it is to cook for others and no, you will not find joy in being your own "special friend" by decorating your solitary tray table with a different flower every night of the week. A few years of living alone and your dining table will either be your lap top, your mattress or a shelf in the refrigerator as you stick a fork in the remnants of take homes of evenings past.

As much fun as it is to entertain, there are some pitfalls you must be on guard for or you will wind up maniacally pitching your pots out the window at small mammals until the proper authorities are called. We all know about not serving too much booze, not inviting people who tend to claw one another's eyes out, having enough hangers and ice and — for the always prepared —

condoms. I am going to take you one step beyond those Betty Crocker list of tips to highlight the really important pitfalls of hosting.

One problem with entertaining is that it quickly becomes an aching duty that whines and hangs on you forever. For years, I had my staff and their families (or whatevers) to my house for a Christmas party. Though I did not make individual Santa hat party favors and fill in the names of each guest in his beard, as recommended by one magazine or plan that sing along around the tree as coaxed by another, they were great parties. Buoyed by the success of the first, I had another and soon came the third and by the fourth year it was now the "annual Christmas party." It was no longer a fun idea — it was another "holiday duty." I started to pity the elf who has to clean up after those hated "reindeer games."

I knew I had been at it too long when I split open my finger while deboning a chicken at 3 in the morning. I was so sleepy, I actually thought my pinky was the thigh bone of the poor beast. This party was now hanging onto my arm every December demanding that I do it better than I did its sister past. I started to dread this favorite time of the year. After returning from the Emergency Room, I knew it was time to stop with the Big Holiday Party.

Another big problem with entertaining is that most well brought up people think they have to extend the same courtesy back to you. No matter how much you protest, they will start to feel embarrassed by not being able to pay you back in kind. That's great — terrific. It's just that I don't always want to go to everyone's house. It isn't anything personal, I just have to feel comfortable in habitats before I can really enjoy myself and you have to spend half the night getting comfortable and then dinner is over and then you have to start worrying about the after dinner "bright and interesting" conversation part.

My friend Henry fixed this problem in his own inimitable style. One of the great cooks of all time, Henry has had about nine close friends over for dinner ever Sunday night for the past thirty years. Yet he refuses ninety percent of their return invitations. A unique fellow he, Henry is part Julia Child, part 18th century sailor who will cook you the most elegant of French meals and serve it buffet style in his stocking feet. If anyone starts to feel insulted about his failure to show at their house he booms out, "I am still going to cook and goddammit if you want to eat come over, if not somebody else will get two damn servings, so suit your self." Unfortunately, in order to pull this off, you need a great deal of charm and gastronomic talent and my tank is about three quarts low on both accounts.

You may have to find your own way to stop the dreaded reciprocity cycle. I have learned to invite only good friends whom I can visit and still feel at home. Less is more in this arena unless you enjoy twittering around like Ivana Trump at the height of "the Season".

There is another type of person for whom you must be on the look out. This is the Habitual Inviter who just happens to have five or ten or fifty other people lying around the house when it is time to come to your party so they just drag them along too. At one of my first big parties I was expecting ten people. Being Italian, I cooked for fifteen, being Sicilian, I added an extra handful in each pot. (It is a well known fact that if Italians don't have enough left overs to feed the population of the basin of the Yellow River, some horrid evil will befall them. It has something to do with a curse and Marco Polo being caught in a compromising position with Kublai Khan's chef. But I am not sure of the details.)

Everything was going along great until in walked the Habitual Inviter with her eight housemates. Of course, it was a sit down dinner with the table preset. I did some scrambling and covered my tracks. It was amazingly easy to convince the guy from accounting that the dog bowl was the first piece in my new ultramodern scooped dinner plate collection. Still, it could have been a disaster, so be careful and check references before you send out those invitations.

The most important thing is to settle into a pattern that suits whatever it is that passes for your lifestyle. Now my vast social schedule consists of calling a few friends now and then and asking them what they have planned that year. If we can find a night that we can meet, we do it, if not we try again later. I still dig out the recipes and dust off the pasta maker but the days of planned, prearranged, "must have" parties is over (although it was a heart breaker giving up the predawn Groundhog Day Brunch).

Entertaining is great now that I have learned (A) not to make it a chore, (B) to invite who I want regardless of social protocol, (C) experiment with fun foods and have the pizza delivery man on call just in case of a disaster and (D) work on a whim.

For a really no strings attached entertaining gift, when the mood strikes me to go all out, I prepare a dinner party and drop it off at the local retirement home. I'm not bucking for sainthood, it's just that odds are the residents won't be able to remember to invite me back.

20

Giving the Gifts That Don't Keep Giving You a Headache

learn to give before it really hurts

～

It 'tis better to give than to receive but not when you have to give "requirement gifts". Because my father was in business for himself, I learned early who was a "requirement gift" recipient — the good customer, the guy who slipped you extra business, the guy who opened or shut his eyes at the right moment. You catch my drift. As a child it was a joy to sort and wrap these gifts, when I became an adult, it became a chore more dreadful than cleaning under the kitchen sink.

For years, I gave clients requirement gifts at Christmas, thus destroying the meaning of the Season and causing me, in a few cases, to spend good money on people whose flesh I wished to rip off in tiny painful pieces. Still, I was afraid not to give them a token fearing that they would remember this when approached by another travel agency. I could just envision the scene. "She gave me good service, low fares but no fruit cake...we will go with your agency from now on." Most clients were decent people and I didn't mind giving some seasonal token of thanks. It just galled me to have to be so charitable to the penny pinching, irritating legends in their own minds who turned every phone call into a coin toss that would decide if I would become a mass murderer or resident of a home for dribbling fools.

Then something happened one year — call it my own personal "Christmas Carol" without the ghosts and (thank God) Tiny Turkey. Two of my clients — the most annoying of the pack — deserted me. One, left my services because his mistress decided to play travel agent. (She overran the budget by several thousand dollars but hey they got to travel together for free without anyone knowing...or so they thought. I am glad that the same person who told me this also shared the revelation with the wife's lawyer.) The other client tried to get out of paying me $7,000 dollars and got very huffy over my silly desire to collect the money.

What really irked me was that, because these two were the scourges of humanity, I had always given them the best Christmas presents. I was afraid to make them angry. When they were both gone, not only was my life happier, I realized that rotten people will do rotten things no matter how virtuous we are to them. From then on it was gifts only to the nice guys. I felt as liberated as old Scrooge himself although I didn't make an ass out of myself by dancing around the house. I merely went to Nordstroms and bought an extra pair of shoes with the money I had saved.

Buoyed by this feeling, I took another emancipating step and vowed to give gifts only to those relatives who didn't make me want to go into a corner and mumble to myself. This was difficult because I have a mother who is the keeper of the great books of life. She can tell you how much every person has ever given at every wedding, shower and funeral since her family smashed into Lady Liberty in New York Harbor. Since childhood I assumed everyone kept detailed logs on this most important issue and that friendships and families rose and fell on such matters.

The first time I refused to buy a birthday gift for the relation who galled my left kidney the most, I waited for the Earth to open and the wind to stop. Nothing happened...life went on...the Earth stayed on its axis...wars did not erupt...pestilence did not consume the neighborhood cats. I got more brazen and went to the next step. I stopped putting a limit on the amount I was going to spend on each gift. There would be no more of, "Let's see, you bought me a twenty dollar gift so I can't buy you that $40 CD Rom set." Nope, I matched the person with the gift that grabbed me the most and left the sales slip tallying to the clerks.

I knew my cure was complete when I stopped keeping emergency gifts on hand. Nothing used to throw me more than to get a holiday gift from someone I didn't have on my list. One year I spent several hours at my own Christmas party trying to find, wrap and inconspicuously deliver something — anything — to a woman who unexpectedly brought me a bottle of cologne. The first problem was that I had forgotten I had purchased so many emergency items and I almost wound up hospitalized with a broken thorax when I discreetly opened the attic only to have them all pour out on me.

I realized I was really doing something that violated the laws of Nature when, in my haste and pain, I accidentally wrapped the "emergency children's gift" instead of the adult model. There she sat cooing and ahing over a box a Crayola crayons and ten coloring books. (It was, after all, the new box with those fun '90s colors included — pretty impressive stuff. It still made for a queasy stomach moment.)

That was the final blow (literally). I would be a gift slave no longer. Now I greet unexpected gifts with a smile and thank you instead of sheer panic. What a wonderful feeling to buy what you want, when you want and for whom you want. If the person feels upset or snubbed by my actions, too bad. The way I look at it now, if I cared that much about what they had to say about me, I would have bought them a gift in the first place.

21

Questions of Life for Which There Will Never be Answers

don't waste your time... these would stump Plato

〜

There are just some great questions of life that no one will ever be able to answer fully and logically so you just might want to get used to that now. These are queries so obtuse, so magnificent in their complexity that they would baffle the brain of Plato, Socrates, Einstein or even Alfred E. Neuman. If you find yourself spending hours pondering any one of these, STOP and move on to working on some puzzle you can crack — like the mystery of the Sphinx (or that of Sam Donaldson's hair.)

1. Why is it that the same Congress that speech-ifies with great abandon against drug deal-ers who hook and kill our children, turn the other face to wine, dine, golf and sleep with those fine representatives of the tobacco lobby, who target our children for those fun filled addictive, cancer causing cigarettes, and the gun lobby, who say with a straight face that you need an assault weapon to blow away a bunny? Why do these same saviors of our future generations also make special deals with meat and poultry lobbyists so they can soak our food supplies in every form of gunk known to Earth?

2. Why is it that no matter who they might step on, sleep with or slash (or step on and slash while sleeping with) to get to "the top", the minute someone gets "famous" for any reason, all previous sins are forgotten and they might eventually get a "humanitarian" award?

3. Why is it that people who have the money get all the unpaid perks? Doesn't anyone think it would thrill her to her knee-highs if a little old lady in Dubuque got a free sub-scription to her favorite magazine — even if it is a nostalgic look at Mamie Eisenhower's spit curls?

4. Why do television weather people have to be perky?

5. Why do many of the world's religions based on a man who preached peace, brotherhood and unity take great glee in terrorizing the stuffing out of their members with fire, brimstone and fear?

6. Why can't some people get it through their thick skulls that our "miserable, do nothing" political system is a direct reflection on their own indifference?

7. Why would someone sit down and actually invent something as heinous as plastic wrap?

8. Why doesn't anyone do more than just complain about our educational system that turns out more than its fair share of kids who don't know an atom from Adam?

9. Why are families the undisputed silk that hold people and society together and also one of the main causes of nervous body tics?

10A. What would life be like if we didn't have lights in our refrigerators?

10B. Do dishes really dance around in the closet when we leave the house?

11. Who decided that we must cover certain parts of our bodies that are "private" while others are perfectly acceptable for human eyes? Can you image what it would be like if noses were obscene? Jimmy Durante would never have gotten out of jail.

12. What magic power is there in female blonde hair that enables it to fascinate and intoxicate males for miles around?

13A. Why aren't more people given the talent to ask the question "why?"

13B. More importantly, why are some of us hooked on making lists?

14. Is this how Larry King got started?

22

The Early Years Are Not The Best Time of Your Life

how not to peak at 18

~

When I was in college I shared a cab with a woman with whom I was having a fairly forgettable conversation until I mentioned that I was a student. She looked at me with a spooky kind of longing and said reverently, "Oh, how I wish I were back in school." I had to fight the urge to jump out of the cab as it careened around the next curb.

Her statement made as much sense to me as someone saying they wished they had four infected wisdom teeth. "Are you for real? People telling you what to do, where to be, how to fill out papers...I can't wait to be free of all of that."

"Oh no, as long as you can make the grades, you have so little responsibility. I wish I could have stayed in school. High school and college are the best years of your life."

We have yet to coin the scientific term for her ailment, but it was clear to me that this was one sick puppy. She reminded me of those kids who sobbed at high school graduation because they just knew it was all down the porcelain facility from there. I mean, what can be left in life after four years of pep rallies and German Class?

If you are in those tender decades of life, and unless you found the cure for cancer in your gym locker, you better hope that your personal best is on the way. High school years, college years, even your entire '20s decade should not be your most triumphant years! That is an old wives tale started by a bunch of cheerleaders who peaked at eighteen. The best part of life is not at the beginning of the parade when your body is out of control, sex brings more fear than thrill, you have no clue what you stand for, your independence is pretty much nonexistent, your voice squeaks and your skin cracks. If that were true, Mankind would have made it a sacred ritual to have everyone toss themselves into an ocean at thirty.

The reason we decide to hang around is that the good part doesn't start until you dance around the block with life a while, feel comfortable in your skin, have a few hard knocks under your belt and learn what is really important...like rainy Saturdays in New York and Daffy Duck cartoons.

Fellow Baby Boomers, take heart. The nice thing about the good part is that it can start at any age, once you realize you have the power to make it happen. So even if you think you are over the hill, for goodness sakes, stop salivating over the dreams of yesteryear and everything lost to the mists of history because the bad part about the good part is that, unlike the memory of the bad parts of youth, it can go away in an instant.

So don't miss the good, thinking about the bad and get on with it...go ahead...put the book down and GO! Now that wasn't so bad was it?

Good.

JOAN PORTE (who doesn't use her middle initial to be trendy but because it is "E" and she cringes when people call her "Joanie") has many labels...successful executive, entrepreneur, lecturer and publisher/editor of the nationally distributed consumer action newsletter, "Porte's Retort: Guide For the Irritated Citizen." This combines her wry sense of humor with solid advice based on the knowledge she gained slaving away on a Political Science degree from the George Washington University in Washington, D.C. and as a Congressional aide, lobbyist and political action committee director (before her redemption and cleansing in waters curing Potomac Fever.)

When she isn't tilting at windmills and the occasional political or corporate bureaucrat or two, Joan serves as a Director of the Card Pal Program, her very serious undertaking to bring some happiness into the lives of lonely Americans.

I need your help with my next book!

Tales of Bombastic
& Bumbling Bureaucrats

Write me in care of the publisher with your favorite stories of the thickest, rudest or most obnoxious bureaucrats you have encountered (or read about in your local paper).

Don't let all that good humor go to waste.

Sorry, I can't publish anonymous stories but I will withhold your name in the book upon request.

ORDER FORM

To order additional copies of this book to distribute as an inspirational guide to others beating a path through the jungle of life, check your bookstore or send $9.95 plus $3.00 shipping and handling to:

Scorpio Press
4301 North Fairfax Drive — Suite 190
Arlington, Virginia 22203

Prices may change without notice.